MEMOIRS OF THE REVOLUTION IN BENGAL

First published 1760
This edition published by Lector House in 2024

ISBN: 978-93-6138-100-3
Edition copyright © 2024 by Lector House LLP
All rights reserved under the International Copyright Conventions.

Lector House LLP
Registered Office: H. No. 96, Block C, Tomar Colony,
Burari, Delhi – 110084, India
info@lectorhouse.com
www.lectorhouse.com

MEMOIRS OF THE REVOLUTION IN BENGAL

WILLIAM WATTS

2024

LECTOR HOUSE
LECTOR HOUSE LLP

MEMOIRS OF THE REVOLUTION IN BENGAL,

ANNO. DOM. 1757.

By which MEER JAFFEIR was raised to the Government of that Province, together with those of *Babar* and *Orixa.*

INCLUDING

The Motives to this Enterprize; the Method in which it was accomplished; and the Benefits that have accrued from thence to that Country, our United Company trading to the *East Indies,* and to the *British Nation.*

Preface.

THE Success that has every where attended the Efforts of the *British* Arms, during the Course of this just and necessary War, will render this Period of our History resplendent, even to latest Ages. It seems, therefore, requisite to give the most accurate and distinct Accounts that can be obtained of these Successes in the remoter Parts of the Globe, that the Nature and Consequences of them may be the better understood here. The People of *Britain* are as well entitled to know, and will with equal Pleasure read, what has been effected for their Service at *Bengal,* as at *Goree*; and accept as kindly the Laurels brought them from *Asia,* as those that come from *Afric* or *America.*

In this we follow only the Custom of other Nations. The *Portuguese* and the *Dutch* have not only general Histories of their Atchievements in the *Indies,* and separate Accounts of their respective Settlements, but numerous Memoirs of particular Expeditions, in which they have been exceeded by the *French.* We should therefore be wanting to ourselves, if, having performed as great Things as they, and having as authentic Vouchers, we should willfully suffer the Memory of them to be lost, and the Merits of our deserving Countrymen swallowed up in Oblivion.

The following Pages will shew, how one of our finest Settlements in the *East Indies* was suddenly sacked and subverted by the Impetuosity of a young Man, intoxicated with Sovereign Power; in what Manner it was recovered and restored; the Peril to which it was again exposed from the same Person; and the Means by which it was not only rescued from a Second Destruction, but the Causes of these Calamities removed; the *British* Interest placed on a more solid Basis than ever; with additional Advantages that were never hoped; so that Stability may be truly said to have been extracted from intestine Troubles, and Public Miseries rendered the Source of Public Safety and Public Benefits.

But as these Wonders could never have been performed but by the Assistance of his Majesty's Fleets and Forces, and as this was derived from the constant and laudable Concern of the Administration, for the Fate of *British* Subjects wherever disposed, it is but a just Tribute of Gratitude to shew how Measures so wisely taken, proved so successful in the Event, that Posterity may profit by the Example, and our Trade ever meet with the like Support, under Officers (if they are to be found) of equal Abilities.

Lastly, it will appear how far the Nation has reaped the Fruits of these signal Events. The Settlement at *Calcutta* being not only effectually restored, but, as far as the Nature of Things will admit, its future Safety as effectually secured, the Honour of the *British* Name repaired, and the Terror of her Arms diffused throughout the *East*. The Fortunes of *British* Subjects, ruined in the first Calamity, unprovided for in the first Treaty, entirely recovered by the Second; many of which being now brought over, are actually vested in the Funds or Lands of *Great Britain*.

Memoirs of the Revolution in Bengal.

THE late Revolution in *Bengal* is so extraordinary in its Nature, of such immediate Consequence to the *East India* Company, and may possibly be of such Importance to the Nation, that a short and perspicuous Relation of this memorable Transaction cannot but be acceptable to the Public. Such a Relation will give a distinct Idea of Things, as to which the World has hitherto had but confused Notions; dispose all Events relating thereto in their proper Places, so that their Motives and Consequences may be clearly understood; and supply those Chasms, that disturb the Order and destroy the Connection between the Narratives which have been written occasionally of particular Points of Fact. Besides, it will explain the Conduct of those who have been chiefly instrumental in bringing such an hazardous, as well as arduous Attempt as this to a happy Conclusion; will shew why it was thought necessary, and on what Account it was originally undertaken; the many, and some of them formidable, Obstacles that were in the Way; and how these were either gradually removed, or gloriously overcome. In a Word, when thoroughly and circumstantially explained, it will open as singular and surprizing a Scene to the View of the inquisitive and judicious Reader, as perhaps he will find in any History respecting our own Times, which, let me have Leave to say, are those that concern us most.

But previous to the Narrative, it will be expedient to give a concise Account of the Inhabitants, and the State of the Government in that Country, where this surprizing Political Catastrophe fell out; and without being well acquainted with which, these succinct Memoirs would not only be less intelligible, but, which is yet worse, would become also very liable to be misunderstood. The Nature of Things depends on their Properties, alike discernable by all who will examine them with equal Care, and with the same Degree of Attention. But the Nature of Facts is determined by the Circumstances that attend them; and if these be not fairly and fully represented, they must be falsely, or at least imperfectly apprehended. In Cases relative to the Alteration of States, a bare Recital of Events establishes only what Alteration they produced, and does not at all inform us to what the Change was owing; gives us no Grounds to conclude, as to the Advantages or Disadvantages flowing from such a Mutation, and does not furnish us with the Means of framing any probable Conjecture as to the Stability or Instability of the New Government.

The two great Nations, inhabiting this Part of the *Indies*, differ widely from each other in their Complexions, Language, Manners, Disposition, and Religion. The *Moguls* (*Moghuls*) who are commonly called *Moors* or *Moormen*, are a robust, stately, and, in respect to the original Natives, a fair People. They speak what the *English* in *India* commonly call the *Moors* Tongue, which is in truth the *Persian*, or at least a Dialect of the *Persian*. They are naturally vain, affect Shew and Pomp in every thing, are much addicted to Luxury, fierce, oppressive, and, for the most part, very rapacious. In respect to Religion, they are *Mohammedans*; the common Sort of the Sect of *Omar* (in which they agree with the *Turks*), but those of Superior Rank are mostly of the Sect of *Ali* (which is followed by the *Persians*), and some affect to be very devout. These have the Dominion, and are possessed of all the Offices of Trust and Power, in virtue of their Descent from the *Moguls*, whose Empire was established by *Timûr*, commonly called *Tamerlane* in this Country; but they are now a very mixed People, composed of *Tartars*, *Arabs*, and *Persians*; more especially of the last mentioned Nation; who for various Reasons have quitted their own Country, but chiefly for the Sake of that Favour and Preferment, which for many Ages they have met with at the Court of (*Dehli*) *Delly*. The *Gentoows*, or Native *Indians*, are of a swarthy Aspect, as their proper Appellation *Hindu* implies; less warlike but more active and industrious than the *Moors*. They are a mild, subtle, frugal Race of Men, exceedingly superstitious, submissive in appearance, but naturally jealous, suspicious, and perfidious; which is principally owing to that abject Slavery they are kept in by the *Moors*; and their Vices are such as innate Cunning, of which they have a great deal, suggests to counteract those of their Masters. They are divided into several Casts or Tribes, of which the most noble is that of the *Bramins*, and there are also several Casts of these. Their Religion is *Paganism*, gross and absurd among the Vulgar, but not so amongst the wiser and better Sort. These Characters are not drawn through any Spirit of Prejudice or Partiality, but from Experience and Observation, and the Faults of both do not so much arise from any Want of Parts, or Defect in their natural Talents, as from their respective Conditions, and the barbarous Severity and perpetual Instability of their Governments.

The *Mogul*, or, as we commonly call him, the *Great Mogul*, is, according to the Constitution of *Indostan*, if Despotism can with any Propriety be stiled a Constitution, as absolute as a Monarch can be. He is the sole Possessor of Property, the single Fountain of Honour, and the supreme Oracle of Justice. The whole Country belongs to him; all Honours are Personal, are bestowed by his Bounty, and resumed at his Pleasure; his Subjects having no other Laws than the Dictates of his Will. The Omrahs, or Great Lords of his Court, who discharge the high Offices in his Household, exercise the Functions of Ministers of State, or hold superior Commands in his Armies, are all Creatures of his own, and so are the Governors of Provinces, stiled in the Language of the Country *Nabobs*, who have again lesser Governments, to which they appoint, called *Phousdarles*. Thus things actually stood under the long Reign of *Aurengzebe*, and under the short one of his Son; but since the Days of his unfortunate Grandson, *Mohammed Shah*, who was dethroned, and restored by *Thamas Kouli Khan*, the *Moguls* are no more than Shadows of what they were; and their Prerogatives become rather Sounds than Substance. Those Emirs or Nabobs, who govern great Provinces, are stiled Subahs, which imports the same as Lord-Lieutenants or Vice-Roys. These Vice-Roys have ever held their Provinces of the Mogul, by rendering him a yearly Tribute, and furnishing their Contingent of Troops, when demanded for his Service; each of them exacting the like Services from their subordinate Governments; in both the Nabobs and Phousdars were supreme, and executed a kind of Sovereign Authority, subject only to those from whom it was delegated, and by whom it might be again taken away when they thought fit. But now they affect a kind of Independence, send their Tribute to Court when they esteem it convenient, and that is but seldom: and devolve their Employments on their Heirs, who having immediate Possession of the Means, find no great Difficulty in getting themselves confirmed, by making proper Presents at *Delly*. If the Mogul attempts to depose any of them, the Person to whom he gives the Commission must raise an Army, and force a Passage to the Government bestowed upon him with his Sword. The same thing happens with regard to the Phousdars, removed by the Suba's; and hence the Confusions that ensue, whenever the Pretenders to the same Post (who are also sometimes supported, as their Interest leads them, by the different trading Nations upon the Coast) to gratify their Ambition, create implacable, ruinous, and endless civil Wars.

As to the *Gentoows*, though Multitudes of them live in the Cities and Provinces governed by the Officers of the Mogul, yet in the mountainous Countries, and in some others, there are many who still maintain their Freedom, or rather are Slaves to Princes of their own, stiled Rajahs, amongst whom the Mahah Rajah, or King of the Marattes, is the most powerful. His Subjects inhabit the Mountains to the South-East of *Goa*, and he has sometimes brought Armies of one Hundred, and sometimes of two Hundred Thousand Men into the Field, composed mostly of Horse. These, as well as the Troops of the lesser Rajahs, of whom there are many, are employed chiefly in predatory Expeditions, and by making very rapid Incursions, and no less rapid Retreats, do a great deal of Mischief in a very little time. This has induced some of the wisest amongst the Mogul Governors to consent to the Payment of an annual Tribute, stiled the Chout, amounting to a fourth Part of the Revenue of the Province, to prevent these Inroads. The Nabobs likewise frequently entertain the Troops of these Rajahs in Pay, in order to increase the Strength of their own Armies. From this concise Account of Things, it will sufficiently appear, that the Power of the Mogul is rather nominal than real; that a kind of Anarchy reigns through the Country; and that where there is any Thing that resembles ever so imperfectly a Form of Government, it has Force for its Basis, is supported by Fraud, and that in

Fact there is hardly any such thing as legal Authority subsisting in any Part of the Empire; so that to measure the Rectitude of Men's Actions in such a Country as this, and in relation to such Governors as these, by the same Rules that take Place under regular Establishments, where Laws are settled and known, and where Justice is duly administred, is not at all founded either in Reason or Equity.

The English established their Presidency at *Calcutta*, towards the Close of the last Century, in virtue of a Phirmaund (Firmân) from the famous *Aurengzebe*, who much extended the Bounds of the Empire on this Side. His Firmân was confirmed, and the Privileges of the *East India* Company much augmented by his great Grandson *Mohammed Furruksîr*. It is therefore indubitable, that having these Concessions made to them in the most ample and honourable Manner, and when the *Mogul* Empire was in its most flourishing Condition, the *English* Nation had as firm and solid a Right to their Possessions and Immunities as that Constitution could give. They were not therefore certainly to be disturbed or controuled by the Governor of the Province, while they behaved themselves peaceably and properly towards him.

The Company and the Servants of the Company had strictly observed the Terms upon which they were bestowed, and were so modest, or rather so cautious, as to keep much within the Bounds of those Concessions, and chose rather to wave some of their Rights than run the Hazard, under so unsettled a Government, of affording any Colour of Complaint. The same Spirit prevailed; the same Care was taken in all the Factories subordinate to this Presidency. When Injuries were done them, they applied to the Suba's for Relief; when the Officers of those Vice-Roys, either with or without their Knowlege, ventured upon Exactions, they proceeded by Remonstrance. If this had its Effect, they thought themselves happy; if not, they bore it with Patience, of which many Instances might be given. They knew very well that Trade was their Business, and that Disputes with the Country Government must be detrimental to their Interests; and therefore studied to avoid them. That this was really the Case, that they had no ambitious Views, that they had not the smallest Intention to perplex or to interfere with the late Suba, appears to Demonstration, from his not attempting to fix any such thing upon them; and still more so, from the Condition in which he found them.

The old Suba of the three Provinces of *Bengal*, *Bahar*, and *Orixa*, who had advanced himself, and seized that Dignity in the usual Way, by a fortunate Audacity, sticking at nothing to gratify his Thirst for Power, *Aliverdy Cawn*, died much advanced in Years, *April* the 9th, 1756, and was succeeded by his adopted Son *Suraja Dowlat* (*Sur Rajah al Dowlat*) who began his Administration with Acts of Violence, and Breach of Faith to some of his own Family; and by that time he had been a Month in Possession of the high Office he assumed, manifested his Aversion to the *English*.

On what his Resentment to the *British* Nation was founded, he was himself at a Loss to say; and the trivial, inconsistent, and in various respects ill-grounded Pretences, he afterwards suggested, as the Motives to his Conduct, evidently shew they were contrived rather to hide, than to declare the Intentions from which he really acted. It has been asserted, and very probably not without sufficient Foundation, that some who knew his violent and rapacious Disposition, made their Court to him, by representing, that the *Europeans* settled in the Provinces he possessed were immensely rich; that he might well expect considerable Sums from them to merit his Favour and Protection upon his Accession to the Government; that he had a Force much more than was adequate to the crushing them absolutely, if he so pleased; that by compelling them, under Colour of their coming as Merchants only into *Indostan*, to desist from raising any new Fortifications, he would have them always at his Mercy; and that in order to succeed effectually, and with little Trouble, he should, to prevent their making it a common Cause, break only with one Nation at a time; and first with the *British*, who could pay him best, and whose Submission would prove an effectual Precedent to the *French* and *Dutch*. It is not unlikely, that the Authors of this Advice might also undertake to negotiate a Compromise at a proper Juncture. This, however, is certain; that, before he proceeded to Hostilities, he had determined to reduce *Calcutta*, and had taken all his Measures for that Purpose, and disposed his Instruments properly with that View.

Cassimbuzar being situated, as it were, at his Door, was of course the first attacked. He caused the Place to be invested on the Twenty-second of *May*, by a numerous Body of Troops, and then invited Mr. *Watts*, who was Chief of the Factory, to a Conference, upon a Safe-Conduct. As the Place (in the Opinion of the best Judges) was indefensible, and if it had been defensible, was without a Garrison; as in point of Ceremony it was the usual Custom for the Chief of that Factory to compliment every new Suba on his assuming that Office, and Mr. *Watts* had all imaginable Reason to hope a good Reception, he accepted that Invitation, and went to the Suba's Camp, where, contrary to his Faith, and in Breach of those Engagements which are in that Country held sacred, he seized and detained him, till by pursuing the same Conduct, and intermixing Fraud and Force against those who had not the Means, and perhaps were doubtful whether they had any Authority to resist, he possessed himself of *Cassimbuzar*, on the fourth of *June*, and then made no farther Secret of his Design to deprive the *English* of all their Settlements, to which, according to the Constitution of the *Mogul* Empire, they had a much better Right than he had to his Dominions. Thus the Troubles of *Bengal* were begun by him in whose Ruin they ended.

This Step taken, his next Enterprize was directly against *Calcutta*; to reduce which, the Suba marched with an Army of Seventy thousand Men, and, when he became Master of it, acted with a Degree of insolent Cruelty, of which the World is too well apprized already, to need any Detail of it here. Let it suffice then to say, that the Suba wreaked his Malice, for Vengeance it could not be stiled, upon a Multitude of innocent People, who had never given him the smallest Offence. Having destroyed the Place, recalled, and then again dispersed the Inhabitants, and with the same lawless Violence extorted large Sums from the *French* and *Dutch* Factories, that he might seem to manifest a general Distaste to *Europeans*, he returned to *Muxadavad* in Triumph.

He had full five Months from this Period to recollect himself, and to consider the Effects of these bold and arbitrary Proceedings, and in which he might have concerted either the Means of restoring the Peace of the Province, or of fortifying his own Strength in such a manner as to be able to make Head against all his Enemies; for he began to find, that besides those this wanton Exercise of his Power had excited, he had several amongst such as had been subject to the Authority, and even sincerely attached to the Person of his Predecessor. But his extreme Haughtiness, and his perpetual Suspicions, joined to the natural Mutability of his Temper, and Want of Experience, being a very young Man, rendered him equally incapable of correcting past Errors, or of digesting any well-connected Plan, and supporting it with that Firmness, without which Success is not to be expected. Sometimes obstinate, mostly irresolute, he forfeited equally the Esteem of Foreigners and Neighbours; and by an unaccountable Compound of Fickleness and Severity, lost the Confidence of all, and excited the Secret Hatred of most of those who were about him.

On the Fifth of *December* Admiral *Watson* anchored with his Squadron in *Ballasore* Road, to which Place Mr. *Watts* and Mr. *Becher*, both Gentlemen of the Council, were sent to congratulate his Arrival, and to acquaint him with the Situation of their Affairs; Mr. *Watts* having been released by the Nabob in *July*. Ten Days after the Squadron arrived at *Fulta*, where, without Loss of Time, Measures were concerted for retrieving the Honour of the *English* Nation, and restoring the Affairs of the Company. The Force was not great, but it was directed by Men of determined Courage, and of distinguished Capacities. Admiral *Watson*, and the Commander in Chief of the Land Forces, Colonel *Clive*, who, after performing Wonders in other Parts of the *Indies*, came to perform still greater Wonders here, and brought with him a Reputation that abundantly supplied the Want of Numbers. On the Twenty-eighth, the Fleet proceeded up the River. On the Twenty-ninth, Colonel *Clive* landed; and the very next Day, with the Assistance of the Squadron, made himself Master of the Fort of *Busbudgia*; which, though a Place of great Strength, if it had been well defended, was taken with little Loss, and proved the happy Omen of all the mighty Things which afterwards followed.

On New-Year's-Day, 1757, some of his Majesty's Ships cannonaded the Batteries, which had been constructed by the Enemy for the Defence of *Calcutta*, where they had a considerable Force; and this with such Success, that when the Troops debarked, they were abandoned. On the Second, the *English* re-possessed themselves of their demolished Settlement; finding in the Fort, as they had done on the Batteries, a numerous Artillery left behind, by those, who had not either Skill or Courage to use them. After this Success, it was resolved to proceed up the River to *Hughley*, a very populous Town, full of Warehouses and Magazines; and in that, as well as other respects, a Place of Consequence; and so much the safer from our Naval Force, as it could not be reached by large Ships. On the Fifth, Captain *Smith* in the *Bridgewater*, and the Sloop of War, anchored within Reach, and fired warmly upon the Town; and being seconded by all the armed Boats in the Fleet, it was very soon reduced. The better to distress the Enemy, the more to alarm the Province, and to work upon the Suba's governing Passion, Fear; Orders were given, though with much Reluctance, for burning the Houses, and for destroying, particularly, all the Magazines on both Sides of the River; which Orders were very punctually executed, and thereby speedily produced the desired Effects.

Both Vice-Admiral *Watson* and Colonel *Clive* had written, towards the Close of the preceding Year, in as civil and polite Terms to the Suba, as the Circumstances of Things would allow, with a View to bring about a Treaty. But that Prince, who had an Army about him, and whose Resentments ran as high as ever, was either not inclined, or did not care to shew an Inclination, to come to any Terms. It was this, that made the Expedition to *Hughley* requisite; and upon the Loss of that, and the Supplies he had there, his Confidence immediately abated, and he condescended to answer the Letters, affirming that he had already written, but that he had Reason to believe, those Letters had not been delivered. Yet even now, when he found it was necessary to offer a Negotiation, and to express a Willingness to reinstate the Company in their Factories, he added, as if requisite to support his Character, that if the *English* thought they could reap greater Benefits by pursuing the War, they might still proceed in their military Operations; as if, by this Appearance of Indifference, he could conceal the Terror he was under, from what had already happened. To support this Air of Intrepidity, he made, at the same Time, a Motion with his Army towards *Calcutta*.

Colonel *Clive* having communicated these Proposals to the Select Committee, entrusted with the Management of the Affairs of the Factory, they sent Messieurs *Walsh* and *Scrafton*, as Deputies, to the Camp of the Suba, who, either deceived by this into an Opinion that he was still formidable to the *English*, or desirous of imposing upon the Deputies, behaved towards them with such a Mixture of Haughtiness and Contempt, as gave little Hopes of their making any great Progress in their Business; and therefore, after some Delay, the Vice-Admiral and the Colonel were obliged to resume their former Measures, and to think of making a fresh Impression on the Suba, that might convince him, he had as much to dread from the Land-Forces as the Fleet. In order to this, it was concerted, that a Detachment of Seamen, commanded by Captain *Warwick*, should land and join the Army, and that Colonel *Clive* should then force the Nabob's Camp. The Captain accordingly debarked, upon the Fifth of *February*, about One in the Morning: At Two they came up with the Forces, which were under Arms. By Three, every Thing was in Order, and they began to move towards the Enemy; the Sailors attending the Train, which consisted of Six Field Pieces, and one Haubitzer. About Five, the Action began, and the Artillery playing on the Right and Left, Colonel *Clive* marched his Troops directly through the Camp of the Suba; though he had between Forty and Fifty thousand Men, and obliged him, with great Loss, to dislodge, and even to abandon some of the Posts that he took after his Retreat; and this, with very little Detriment to his very small Army, not above Forty Men being killed, and not so many as Seventy wounded. This brisk Attack, seconded by a Letter from Vice-Admiral *Watson*, intimating, that this was a Specimen only of what the *British* Arms, when provoked, could perform, answered the Intention perfectly. The Suba immediately desired to renew the Negotiation, which went on with such Alacrity, that it was concluded and signed upon the Ninth, by which an end was put to a War, that had subsisted about Nine Months. This Treaty was conceived in the following Terms.

I. Whatever Rights and Privileges the King has granted the *English* Company, in their Phirmaund, and the Hushulhoorums sent from *Delly*, shall not be disputed, or taken from them; and the Immunities therein mentioned, be acknowleged and stand good.

Whatever Villages are given the Company by the Phirmaund, shall likewise be granted, notwithstanding they have been denied by former Subahs. The Zemindars of those Villages not to be hurt or displaced, without Cause.

Signed by the Nabob, in his own Hand.

I agree to the Terms of the Phirmaund.

II. All Goods passing and repassing through the Country, by Land or Water, with *English* Dusticks, shall be exempt from any Tax, Fee, or Imposition whatever.

I agree to this.

III. All the Company's Factories, seized by the Nabob, shall be returned. All Monies, Goods, and Effects, belonging to the Company, their Servants and Tenants, and which have been seized and taken by the Nabob, shall be restored; what has been plundered and pillaged by his People, made good by the Payment of such a Sum of Money, as his Justice shall think reasonable.

I agree to restore whatever has been seized and taken
by my Orders, and accounted for in my Sincary.

IV. That we have Permission to fortify *Calcutta*, in such Manner as we may think proper, without Interruption.

I consent to this.

V. That we shall have Liberty to coin Siccas, both of Gold and Silver, of equal Weight and Fineness with those of *Muxadavad*, which shall pass in the Provinces.

I consent to the English *Company's coining their own Imports of Bullion and Gold into Siccas.*

VI. That a Treaty shall be ratified, by Signing and Sealing, and swearing to abide by the Articles therein contained; not only by the Nabob, but his principal Officers and Ministers.

I have sealed and signed the Articles, before the Presence of God.

VII. That Admiral *Watson* and Colonel *Clive*, on the Part and Behalf of the *English* Nation, and of the Company, do agree to live in a good Understanding with the Nabob, to put an End to these Troubles, and to be in Friendship with him, while these Articles are performed and observed by the Nabob.

I have sealed and signed the foregoing Articles, upon these Terms, that if the Governor and Council will sign and seal them, with the Company's Seal, and will swear to the Performance on their Part, I then consent and agree to them.

In this Treaty, the intelligent Reader will see, there were Three great Points sufficiently explained, to shew the Injustice and Oppression of the Suba, in his Attack upon the *English* Settlements, even upon Reflection in his own Opinion, tho' far from being as conclusive in respect to the Remedies and Indemnifications, that, in consequence of so full a Declaration, were to be procured. The First regarded the Possessions, Immunities, and Privileges, conceded to the *East India* Company, by the Royal Phirmaund, which *Suraja Dowlat* acknowleged to have violated, promised Restitution, and undertook, in the most solemn Manner, not to invade them again. But as this was conceived only in general Terms, these Rights, and the Limits of their respective Possessions, required a thorough Discussion. The next was, as to the Fortifications of *Calcutta*; the Legality and Expediency of which he now admitted in their utmost Extent, as being plainly necessary to the Security of the Place, the *British* Inhabitants, and even of the *Mogul*'s Subjects, living under its Protection; and to this was added, the Coinage of their own Imports, in Gold and Silver, to which they had always a Right, though it had not been exercised. The last was, the full and immediate Compensation, which he stipulated, for all the Damages the Company, and those dependent upon it, had sustained; but which he contracted only to make, so far as the Produce of the Plunder should appear to have come into his Hands. It was evident, therefore, that, though in Words and in Appearance much had been obtained by the Peace, this still depended, in a great Measure, as to the most material Part, the Performance, on the proper Settling of these Articles, and the Liquidation of the Damages, in reference to which, the Sincerity of the Suba's Intention, and his Readiness to execute what he had undertaken, was almost the sole Security. In order to adjust these Points, without which the Treaty was of very little Consequence to those ruined and undone by the War, the Select Committee very properly made choice of Mr. *William Watts*, who had been their Chief at *Cassimbuzar*, who was one of the Members of that Committee, a Person well known to the Nabob, and who had been, as the Suba himself owned, the first innocent and causeless Victim to his Resentment, or rather Caprice. His Acceptance of this Commission, by which he was again to put himself into the Power of this unsteady Prince, in so critical a Conjuncture, and charged with so troublesome and intricate a Negotiation, was a very full Proof of his Fidelity to, and Zeal for, the Interests of the Company; as it likewise was an evident Testimony of the good Opinion of his Associates; who, upon mature Deliberation, invested him solely with so great a Trust.

He was, indeed, in every respect, fittest for this Employment (had there been any Competitor); an Employment, by far the weightiest, and of the most Consequence, of any in *Bengal*. He had been many Years in the Country; was well acquainted with the Language, as well as accustomed to the Manners and Disposition of the Inhabitants; was much esteemed, and had many Connections with them. He understood their Politics also, at least as much as such fluctuating Politics as theirs could be understood; the true Interest of the Province, and the Constitution of *Indostan* in general, and the State of the neighbouring Governments in particular. Besides, he was personally known to all the Ministers, and had received very singular Marks of Esteem from the Suba himself. Add to all this, that the Company, in case of the Death or Resignation of Mr. *Drake*, had appointed this Gentleman to the Government of *Calcutta*, which, taken together, proves, that this Choice was not the Work of Chance or Favour, but proceeded from mature Deliberation, and a just Regard to the Consequence of that Negotiation, in which he was to be employed.

The Perplexities springing from such a Variety and Complication of Matters that were to be adjusted, the Mutability of the Suba's Nature, and his Want of Judgment and Experience, and the Difficulties naturally arising in settling the Concessions, which had been just extorted from him by Treaty, were not the only Circumstances that embarrassed this Negotiation. The *French*, perfectly well informed of every Step taken or intended, and no less skilled in the Art of Intrigue, had most effectually retained several of those whom the Suba frequently consulted, or chiefly trusted, in their Interest by gratifying them with Presents. They had still a more powerful Tie on them than this, being in Debt Thirteen Lack of Rupees, or upwards of One hundred and Sixty thousand Pounds Sterling, to *Juggut Seat*, the greatest Banker in the Empire of *Indostan*, and the Second in Power in *Bengal*; to whose Advice for many Years past the Subas paid the greatest Attention. They very well knew, that Men might be false to their Benefactors; but they rightly judged, that even the worst of Men, more especially when avaricious, would be true, where they could not possibly be false, without betraying their own Interest. Under Circumstances like these, there was no Probability, indeed there was no Possibility, of so much as attempting any Thing, but in the Mode of the Court; that is, by opposing Corruption to Corruption, making Friends of the Mammon of Unrighteousness, and getting upon even Ground with those, with whom they were obliged to contend.

But in order to understand the whole of this Matter thoroughly, we must consider the State that Affairs were then in, with respect to the two contending Nations. Advice of the breaking out of the War, between *Great Britain* and *France*, arrived in *India*, the very Day after the Treaty was concluded with the Suba; and of course opened a new Scene. From being commercial and political Rivals, we were now become open Enemies; a Circumstance which we were very sure the *French* would improve, and which therefore it was our Duty not to neglect. We had at present a Fleet and an Army; for however small they might be, as Matters stood, they both deserved those Titles, and this gave us great Advantages. On the other Hand, the former was soon to quit the Coast, and perhaps Part of the latter, which was a great Disadvantage. The capital Point, therefore, was to avail ourselves of them, while they remained, so as to settle Things upon a stable Foundation, with regard to the *French*, as well as to the Nabob, before the Season came in which the Fleet was to return. In respect to the former, the Admiral and Colonel *Clive*, with the Assistance of the Select Committee, were to take the best Measures they could; and Mr. *Watts* was to regulate the latter; and his Success, or Want of Success, must have apparently had such an Influence upon the whole, that the Reader most certainly needs not be informed, how much depended upon his Courage, Conduct, and Capacity.

The Interest the *French* had in the Court of the Suba, and their Method of acquiring it, have been already stated. This they would have understood to be barely for their own Support and Security; but however, there were some Surmises, that it was also, and had ever been, not a little to our Prejudice. It was whispered, that the Favour shewn them, in Comparison of the *Dutch*, after the Destruction of our Settlements, when he affected to fine both Nations for augmenting the Works about their respective Factories, was, in Consideration of their having secretly furnished Artillery, when he marched against *Calcutta*. This was a Suspicion in the *Indies*, and as such only is mentioned; but it is very certain, that the Letters wrote Home to *Europe* were entirely in *Suraja Dowlat*'s Favour, containing a very unfair, and, which was much worse, a very plausible, but utterly false Representation of the Grounds of the Quarrel, which was published to our Prejudice in all the foreign Gazettes.

When Mr. *Watts* set out for the Suba's Residence, he was accompanied by *Omichund*, an eminent Merchant of *Calcutta*, who was well known to the Suba, and his Ministers. This Merchant, Mr. *Watts* sent to *Hughley*, to discover, as far as he could, what were the real Intentions of the *Moors*, in case we attacked *Chandenagore*. He returned the next Day, *February* the Eighteenth, with a very distinct Account. He had been informed by *Nuncomar*, the Phousdar, or Governor of *Hughley*, that the very Day before, Two Persons, *Seen Bawboo* and *Montra Mull*, arrived from the Nabob, with a Lack of Rupees, as a Present to the *French* Factory; and also with Orders to the Phousdar, to assist the *French*, if attacked; or if they were the Aggressors, to assist the *English*. Mr. *Watts* was too well acquainted with the Genius of the *Moors*, and the Temper of the Suba, to be deceived by this Shew of Impartiality. He considered the Present as a Declaration in Favour of the *French*; and the Stile of his Orders as calculated to amuse the *English*. *Omichund* was entirely of the same Opinion. Mr. *Watts*, therefore, advised the Select Committee to attack *Chandenagore* without Delay, assuring them, that they had nothing to apprehend from the Resentment of the Suba; that if once the two Nations were engaged in Hostilities, the *Moors* would not come to the Succour of either; and that after all, there were but Three hundred Matchlock Men in *Hughley*. He saw from the Beginning the Mischief that was to be feared; and the only Remedy that could be applied. He therefore very freely pointed out the one, and very warmly recommended the other. It had been a very happy Event, if his Counsel had been then taken.

On the Twenty-first of *February*, in the Evening, Mr. *Watts* arrived in the Camp, and had his Audience of the Suba, who embraced him, gave him the strongest Assurances that every thing should be adjusted speedily, and to his Satisfaction; adding a Promise of the Surpau, (Sirrapah) or Vest of Honour, which, however, Mr. *Watts* declined receiving, till they came to *Muxadavad*. He was very soon sensible of the Difficulty of his Task, the Pains he must be at in tracing the Goods taken from their several Factories, the procuring actual Restitution in some Cases, an equitable Equivalent in others; the restoring a free Commerce, which had been stopped, by express Orders, from the very Beginning of the Troubles; and in doing all this, of the almost insurmountable Obstacles that the Mutability of the Suba's Inclinations, the Intrigues of the *French*, the Insinuations of Ministers, swayed solely by their own Interests, would throw in his Way. But he saw, that the true Source of all these Embarrassments was the Suba's Insincerity, and the Scheme he had formed of resuming his Despotism, in regard to the *Europeans*, by borrowing their own Assistance, and playing one Nation against another, till, by the weakening of their Forces in such Disputes, he became too strong for both. His Project was too great for his Capacity; he did what he could to execute it, but it was beyond his Force, and his very manner of managing it defeated his Design.

The public Declarations of this irresolute Prince, were diametrically opposite to the whole Tenor of his Conduct. He had no sooner concluded the Treaty with Us, than he wrote to Admiral *Watson* in the warmest Terms of Friendship, and in a very remarkable Letter to Colonel *Clive* assures him, that our Enemies should be his, as he expected that we should look upon his Enemies as ours; and that he depended upon the Assistance of the *English* for maintaining the future Tranquility of his Dominions. But when Mr. *Watts* communicated to him at large the Reasons that might induce us to reduce the *French* Settlement at *Chandenagore*, he made no Scruple of altering his Language. He then said, he would not suffer the Peace of his Territories to be violated by either Nation; that he would protect both, while they remained quiet; that he would assist the *French* with all his Forces, if we, after this, ever attacked them; and that he would join us in like Manner, if we were attacked by the *French*. All this, however, was far from imposing on those who were at the Head of our Affairs. Mr. *Watts* framed his Precautions so well, that he knew exactly the Measures which the Suba took, or was inclined to take, and gave the most early Intelligence of them to the Select Committee, who, from thence, were well enabled to take their own; by which his Schemes were disappointed without Noise, and without so much as suspecting their having any such Informations; though these came chiefly from his own Head-Spy, who, by an Application these Sort of People rarely can resist, Mr. *Watts* had brought over entirely to the Company's Interests.

By comparing his private Intrigues with some of his more public Transactions, there could not be a Shadow of Doubt left as to his real Intentions, though he always dissembled, and often disavowed them. Immediately after his Treaty with Us, and consequently after he knew that they were our Enemies, he bellowed upon them very conspicuous Marks of

Kindness, and such as could not fail of affording Umbrage to the *English*. He made them, as has been before-mentioned, a Present of a Lack of Rupees in ready Money; he cancelled an Obligation they had given him for twice that Sum; he promised them the Privileges of a Mint; he proposed granting them a very considerable Augmentation of Territory; and even went so far, as to offer them the Possession of the City of *Hughley*. These were Circumstances that indicated their standing much in his good Graces, or that he expected from them Services equivalent to these substantial and extraordinary Benefits. The Truth, as far as it could ever be discovered, was this. They, and his Ministers in their Interest, made him believe their Strength in his Dominions to be very far beyond what it really was. Besides this, they magnified their Successes in other Parts, and took a great deal of Pains to persuade him, that Mr. *Bussy*, with a very numerous Army, was within a little Distance of his Territories, and might either fall upon, or come to his Support against, any Enemy, according as he should behave towards them. These Representations, the Nature of the Suba considered, may in some measure, and only in some measure, account for the Part that he acted.

As Mr. *Watts* was upon the Spot, watched every Motion of the Suba, knew exactly the Character of his Courtiers and principal Ministers, and had the most certain Intelligence of every thing that passed, he continued to represent the Necessity of attacking *Chandenagore*. He saw that, as far as his Timidity would suffer him to go, the Suba was already united to the *French*. He was satisfied that he dealt deceitfully with the *English*; more especially after Mr. *Watts* prevailed on Colonel *Clive* to write to the Suba, in the strongest Terms, that he might confide in him on every Occasion; and that on any Emergency he would march at his Request to his Assistance, against all his Enemies. After this, the Suba never mentioned any Desire or Thoughts of demanding Aid from the *British* Nation. Mr. *Watts* was therefore convinced that we could never gain him; and that, though now he temporized, he waited only a fit Season to act against us, in Conjunction with the *French*, upon whom he was daily heaping Favours, while it was with much Difficulty, and in consequence of repeated Sollicitations, he was ever brought to do common Justice to us. In this Situation Mr. *Watts* exhorted the Admiral, the Colonel, and the Select Committee, not to let slip this favourable Opportunity, and to apprehend nothing from the Suba's Resentment, who would never venture to give them any Succours, or take an open Part in their Favour, or to our Prejudice. But if the Fleet was once gone, and a fair Occasion offered, he would as certainly embrace it, and begin a new War, with as little Scruple as he had done the last, with more Advantage on his Side, and less on ours: Arguments, which, though strong and self-evident, did not meet with general Acceptance.

The Select Committee, though they paid great Deference to the Advice, and had a very just Sense of the Zeal, of Mr. *Watts*, for the Nation and the Company's Service; yet they were very unwilling to venture again upon Hostilities, from a strong Suspicion that the Suba, whether he actually joined the Enemy or not, would suspend the Execution of the Treaty, renew the Interruption of their Trade, and by that Means hinder their Investments for another Year. They knew so well, and dreaded so much, the Consequences that would have inevitably attended such an Event, that, in spite of all Mr. *Watts* could allege, they inclined to a Neutrality. This was an Expedient the Suba had proposed, and was another visible Indication of what were his secret and settled Intentions. The Sentiments, or rather the Sollicitations of the Select Committee, prevailed upon the Admiral and the Colonel to acquiesce in this Plan; insomuch that the latter wrote in very strong and pathetic Terms to the Suba, informing him, that whatever Representations of a contrary Nature he might have received, yet himself was very confident, that his Forces were able to reduce *Chandenagore* in Two days; nevertheless, in consideration of the great Repugnancy he shewed to the disturbing the Tranquility of the Province, he would, out of pure Regard to the Suba's Friendship, consent to such a Neutrality as he proposed, provided it was guarantied by him, and he solemnly undertook to act with all his Forces against that Nation by which it was first infringed.

When Mr. *Watts* saw, that after all he had offered against it, this Point was driven thus far, and that in all Probability it would be speedily concluded, he turned his Thoughts to the giving it still greater Security, and with that View advised, that *Juggut Seat* should undertake for the due Performance of whatever should be agreed upon by the *French*; which, considering the

Influence that his Debt gave him over them, and the high Credit in which he stood with the Suba and his Ministers, appeared to be the only Method of giving to this Measure the utmost Consistency of which it was capable. This shews how perfectly well-disposed Mr. *Watts* was to facilitate any Step taken for the Company's Service, though ever so contrary to his own Opinion; and at the same Time affords a Proof of his thorough Knowlege of Men and Things in that Country, by which he was enabled to devise the Means of rendering this Convention more safe and more effectual, than any that had been proposed by such as had originally planned, and now pressed its Execution. But though he discovered so much Integrity, and so much Abilities in suggesting this additional Strength to a Neutrality, he still looked upon it as diametrically opposite to the Company's true Interest, and as the single Step that could ever put it in the Power of the Suba and the *French*, to bring their deep and dangerous Designs to bear.

But when all seemed to be absolutely settled, and nothing wanting to this Neutrality but the concluding and signing it in Form, the *French* themselves overturned it, by avowing that they had no sufficient Authority to support an Act of that Nature, which might be declared invalid by their Superiors. Mr. *Watts* immediately laid hold on and improved this very unexpected Incident, by representing, in the strongest Light, to the Suba, the Condescension shewn him by the *British* by accepting, and the Indignity offered to him by the *French* in rejecting, his Expedient. This had so great an Effect, that in the first Transport of his Resentment he directed a Letter to be written to Vice-Admiral *Watson*, in which he tacitly permitted the Attack of the *French* Factory, by recommending Mercy to the Enemy when it should be reduced; and desiring the military Operations of the *English* might be conducted with as little Prejudice to his Country, or Disturbance to his People, as it was possible. Mr. *Watts*, who had secured the Suba's Secretary to our Interest, engaged him to pen this important Epistle in a proper Stile, so as to permit the Attack immediately, and to dispatch it without Delay: Precautions, which were of the utmost Consequence, and which, in the Event, gave us all those Advantages we afterwards reaped, and which, through the Blessing of Divine Providence, we still possess in *Bengal*.

As there was great Address used in obtaining this Letter, so it arrived in the most critical Conjuncture. For, notwithstanding the *French* had avowed their Want of Power to conclude an effectual Neutrality, yet so much were some afraid of recurring again to Arms, that they were still for accepting of this Expedient, however precarious. Upon this, Admiral *Watson* held a Council of War, to consider what was most proper to be done; and it was while this Council was actually sitting, wherein those who argued yet for a Neutrality insisted chiefly upon the Suba's Repugnancy to see the Flame of War, so lately extinguished, again rekindled in his Dominions, that this Letter was brought, which cut the Gordian Knot, and put an End to the Debate. How the *French* came to act in this Manner, and by so frank a Declaration defeat the Scheme of the Suba, and run themselves upon Destruction, is not easy to conceive. In all Probability, they did not imagine, that even, after this, we would venture to fall upon them, and they were willing to preserve to themselves, against a proper Season, the Liberty of attacking us; or, which is yet more probable, depended on the Suba's exerting his whole Force, in Case of our besieging them, in their Defence; which would have rendered the Expedition much more difficult. Be this as it will, the Letter defeated all their Schemes; and the Sequel of the Transaction shewed how much better Mr. *Watts* was acquainted with the Disposition of the *Moors*, and more thoroughly Master of the Suba's Temper, and Manner of acting, notwithstanding the Intrigues they had been so long carrying on in his Court, and their having such Connections with his Favourites and Ministers.——— But let us now return from Reflections to Facts, and having clearly stated this very remarkable Stroke of Policy, resume the Thread of our Narrative.

Vice-Admiral *Watson*, Colonel *Clive*, and the Select Committee, came to this final Resolution, in the Beginning of the Month of *March*, and entered with all the Diligence and Dispatch possible on the necessary Preparations for this important Expedition, well knowing that the *French* were not ignorant of their own Danger, or at all remiss or careless in providing against it. *Chandenagore*, the chief of their Settlements in *Bengal*, was a Place very well situated on the Side of the River, Twenty-seven Miles above *Calcutta*, which is a Branch of the *Ganges*, at a small distance below *Hughley*. The Director at this Settlement has under him the *French* Company's Factories of *Cassimbuzar*, *Dacca*, *Patna*, *Jeuda*, and *Ballasore*. They prudently contrived, at the Beginning of the Troubles, to strengthen it with various Outworks and Batteries, had in it a Garrison of Five hundred *Europeans* and Seven hundred *Blacks*, with some Mortars, and near Two hundred Pieces of Cannon mounted. They took the Precaution also to send away some of their Merchandize, and the best Part of their Effects, under Colour of providing the better for their Defence; raised considerable Magazines, which were well provided; and made such Dispositions, and kept so good a Countenance, as imposed upon most of the *Moors*, and perhaps upon some of themselves. As they chiefly feared the Squadron, they sunk Two Ships, a Ketch, a Hulk, a Snow, and a Vessel without Masts, directly in the Channel, within Gunshot of the Fort, and laid Two Booms, moored with Chains, across the River. Besides these, they sunk and ran on Shore Five large Vessels, above the Fort, that they might throw every Impediment possible in the Way of our Squadron. In consequence of these military Operations, which were very judiciously planned, and the best their Circumstances would admit, they resolved to stand the Attack; but whether they had any Hopes given them by the Suba of his Assistance, or whether they relied at all on his Insinuations of Aid, in case they were given, could not be learned; though he actually advanced a Corps of Troops, as we shall see hereafter, which might render such a Conjecture not at all improbable.

A Reinforcement of Three hundred Men from *Bombay* arriving at *Calcutta*, Colonel *Clive* advanced by the River Side, with Seven hundred Whites, and Sixteen hundred Seapoys, towards the *French* Settlement; and with very little Loss took Possession of most of the Out-Posts on the Fourteenth of *March*. On the Fifteenth, the Enemy abandoned all their Batteries, notwithstanding these were very well disposed, and in exceeding good Order. He was now possessed of every Post they had, but the Fort, and a Redoubt seated between the River Side and the Fort Walls, wherein were mounted Eight Pieces of Cannon, Twenty-four Pounders, Four of which pointed down the River. The same Day Admiral *Watson* sailed with the *Kent* of Sixty-four, the *Tyger* and *Salisbury*, each of Fifty Guns, having previously sent a Twenty-Gun Ship, and a Sloop, to cover the Boats attending the Camp. On the Eighteenth, he anchored about Two

Miles below *Chandenagore*, and the Troops on Shore being employed in raising a Battery against the Fort, the Weather becoming extremely foggy, and the Impediments before-mentioned being of Necessity to be removed, occasioned some Delay. The First Thing to be done was clearing the River; and the Booms being cut, and running adrift, a proper Passage was soon discovered, by sounding, and without losing Time in weighing the *French* Vessels. While this was about, the brave Admiral *Pocock*, who was just arrived at *Culpee* in the *Cumberland*, resolving to have a Share in the Action, came in his Long-Boat, and going on board his Majesty's Ship the *Tyger*, hoisted his Flag there. On the Twenty-third, at Six in the Morning, the *Tyger*, *Kent*, and *Salisbury*, weighed. About Ten Minutes after the Enemy began to fire from the Redoubt, but their Artillery was soon silenced by the *Tyger*. Before Seven the Ships were properly stationed, and the Signal being given, the Engagement began; the Firing continuing very brisk on both Sides, till a Quarter after Nine, when the Besieged hung out a Flag of Truce, and the Articles of Capitulation were very quickly settled and signed. In consequence of this, Captain *Latham*, of the *Tyger*, was dispatched by Vice-Admiral *Watson* to receive the Keys of the Fort, into which Colonel *Clive* marched with the Troops about Five in the Afternoon. Thus *Chandenagore*, according to the Scheme originally proposed, constantly insisted upon, and at last rendered practicable by Mr. *Watts*, with all the *French* subordinate Settlements in the Province of *Bengal*, were reduced; and thereby most of the Schemes laid for the future Destruction of *Calcutta*, and the other *English* Factories, rendered abortive. An Expedition, in the first Instance, glorious to the *British* Arms, and in its Consequences, as from the Sequel of this Relation will appear, of the highest Importance.

This signal Advantage was not obtained without some Loss. Admiral *Pocock* was wounded, but not dangerously. The gallant Captain *Henry Speke*, equally distinguished by the Clearness of his Head and the Warmth of his Heart, who commanded the *Kent*, on board which Vice-Admiral *Watson* wore his Flag, received a Wound from a Cannon Shot, which unhappily carried away the Leg of his Son, who deceased soon after, a Youth of the most amiable Character, extraordinary Learning, and admirable Abilities. The first Lieutenant, Mr. *Samuel Perreau*, and the Master of the *Tyger*, were both killed; the Third and Fourth Lieutenants were also wounded; and the former died. Of the private Men there were Thirty-two killed, and One hundred wounded. The Enemy had Forty killed and Seventy wounded in the Fort. They must be allowed to have defended themselves with great Spirit and Resolution, and probably would not have submitted so soon, if they had not suffered severely from Colonel *Clive*'s Batteries, and been still more galled by the Fire of his Men, from the flat Roofs of the Houses, which in Truth made it almost impossible for them to stand to their Guns. A Part of the *French* Troops made their Escape, and marched Northwards, after whom Colonel *Clive* sent a Detachment of Six hundred Seapoys, and Vice Admiral *Watson* ordered several Boats up the River of *Hughley*, to seize upon whatever was *French* Property; notwithstanding which, a great deal of the Company's Effects and Merchandize were concealed and carried away. This Blow was very decisive in reference to the *French*, whose Measures it entirely broke, by rendering the Schemes they had formed, with respect to the Suba, utterly impracticable. On the other hand, it released the *English* from the Apprehensions they were under of being again attacked in *Calcutta*, in case the Squadron had left them without reducing this Place. These were so far from being Suspicions lightly founded, that their Danger was so great and so apparent, considering the Circumstances they were then in, and the Suba's delaying to restore their Artillery, that, if not encouraged by this Event, they would have been very slow in re-settling *Calcutta*. Happy as those immediate Effects were! they were hardly so much as remembred, after the greater Advantages that followed; which demonstrated how justly this Resolution was taken, and in what a critical Conjuncture it was executed.

We have before hinted, that, notwithstanding the Suba had transmitted a Letter of Permission to Vice-Admiral *Watson* to act as he thought proper against the *French*, without which Letter the Admiral and the Colonel would not have proceeded, nay went farther, and recommended them to his Mercy, yet he presently changed his Mind. He desired Mr. *Watts* to write to the Colonel, that he would not have War made in his Country, by which the People under his Government must suffer, the King's Revenues be lessened, and the Tranquility of his Dominions disturbed. The *French*, who had misled him from the Beginning, deceived him to the very last.

They assured him, that, in the first Attack, the *English* had been repulsed with Loss, and gave him to understand, that they did not doubt obliging them to retire. The Suba was so much embarrassed by the contradictory Reports he heard, and looked upon this Transaction to concern him so nearly, that he wrote Letter after Letter to Colonel *Clive*, who is said to have received no less than Ten of them in one Day, and these in very opposite Stiles; which the Colonel answered punctually, with all the Calmness and Complaisance imaginable, expressing great Concern at the Impression which the Calumnies of his Enemies had made on that Prince's Mind, and assuring him of his sincere Attachment, as long as he adhered to the Treaty. At length the Suba grew so very uneasy, that he sent *Mutrumul*, in whom he said he placed great Confidence, to the Colonel, with Orders to act, if there was any room for it, as a Mediator. But the Situation of Things at his Arrival made such a Commission visibly impracticable; which *Mutrumul* perceiving, extolled the *English* highly, and threw all the Blame upon the *French*. To give Weight, however, to this intended Mediation, *Roydoolub* advanced, by his Master's Command, at the Head of Six thousand Men, within a small Distance of *Hughley*. But to prevent this from giving any Umbrage, *Mutrumul*, when the Attack was made, assured the Colonel, that *Roydoolub* had the Suba's Instructions to obey his Orders, which the Colonel took in exceeding good Part, and returned that Prince Thanks for this gracious Offer of his Assistance. The Moment the Place surrendered, he gave Notice of it to the Suba, and ascribed his Success to the Favour of Heaven and his Excellency's Auspice, under which his Arms had been so fortunate. A Compliment, which the Suba knew not how to receive with even a tolerable Grace, or to reject without giving Offence. In reality, he had brought his Affairs by this time into a very perplexed Condition, of which he was sensible, now it was too late; though very probably he might not have Sagacity enough to discern, that the Whole of these Misfortunes had no other Source than the Unsteadiness of his Councils, and the Duplicity of his Conduct. What we have already said will afford Proofs more than sufficient to establish this; but as the setting it in a clear Light will be the best means of explaining the Motives to the Transactions that ensued, we hope the subsequent Remarks will not appear tedious to the Reader.

The Suba, wanting alike in Parts and in Experience, unable to reject bad Counsels, and prone to pursue his own Notions, as far as they could be carried by his Power, shewed plainly from the very Beginning, that he had no formed System; and if he could be stiled so at all, was certainly a bad Politician. His setting out was by breaking at once with all the *European* Nations; which, if their reciprocal Jealousies of each other, and some other Circumstances, had not hindered, must have united them all against him, and that Union would have rendered his Scheme abortive. As this did not happen, it encouraged him to take another wrong Step, by attacking and destroying the *English*, without having so much as a plausible Pretence. This Act of arbitrary Violence visibly subverted the Foundation of his own Scheme, if it ever had any, by proving, in the strongest Manner, that no *European* Nation could subsist as Merchants in his Dominions, without having Places so well fortified, as not to lie at his Mercy. When, therefore, he was reduced to the Necessity of concluding a Treaty, the very Basis of that Treaty was his confessing this last Position to be well founded, and admitting by his own Consent, as the only practicable Grounds of Peace, what he had before laid down as the Reason of his taking up Arms. But when he had done this, and might have been quiet, by adhering constantly to that Treaty, he again mistook his Point. Uniformity of Conduct was so little in his Constitution, that he immediately lost all the Advantages he seemed to have sought by that Measure, and which indeed were clearly asserted to have been the Objects he had in View, in his Letters to Admiral *Watson* and Colonel *Clive*, by shewing a visible Repugnance to the Execution of it in every Step, and doing that slowly and ungracefully, which, if he had done chearfully and at once, might have procured him the Confidence of the *English*, and have thoroughly extricated him from those Difficulties into which his first Errors had plunged him.

His Conduct with regard to the *French* was to the full as inconsiderate, and no less inconsistent. His Kindness, Friendship, or whatever it was towards them, was as fatal as his Aversion or Dislike had been to the *English*, and productive of the very same Misfortunes. He was undoubtedly imposed upon and misled by the fake Impressions he received from them of their Strength: But in this he was inexcusable, as these Representations were grounded only upon vague and uncertain Reports of what they had done, and of what Strength they had in other Parts of the *Indies*, from whence all the Assistance they could give him was to be hoped, and this against a Power, the Weight of which he had already felt; and to say nothing of the Obligation he was under to maintain that Peace he had solemnly confirmed by his Oath, which was still at his very Doors. If he had really intended, as he seemed very desirous it should be believed it was his Intention, to preserve Peace in his Dominions, and to prevent the *English* and *French* from committing Hostilities against each other in them, to the Prejudice of Commerce, in which he was principally interested, and which was also, and was allowed to be, the common Concern of all, he might by acting firmly have carried that Point, by insisting upon a Neutrality under his Guaranty, and a peremptory Declaration that he would stop the Trade, and seize the Effects of that Nation, which violated a Neutrality so concluded; since under this it is certain the *English* would have acquiesced, and, without the Encouragement or Assistance of the Suba, the *French* durst not have broke it. But his Intrigues with them, or, as many thought, a Secret Treaty, encouraged their Director to declare, that he was not vested with Authority to conclude any such Neutrality; and even this, which he always knew, he did not acknowlege, until the Time was lost, in which he might have obtained it from *Pondicherry*; and this plainly put the *English* under a Necessity of exerting the Force then in their Hands without Delay, which ended in the taking *Chandenagore*. Here again, if he had ever had any settled Principle of Action, would have been his Time to have shewn it; for if, upon Colonel *Clive*'s marching, he had assisted the *French* with his whole Force, he might very probably have saved them. But as he had hitherto been all along the Dupe of their Politics, so in this Instance they were the Dupes of his, and were sacrificed to his Want of Steadiness and Spirit. On the whole, therefore, it became evident, that the Suba was more dangerous to his Friends than to his Enemies; and the Hazard of being hurt lay not in opposing, but in placing any Confidence in him. A Lesson, which, as it had been taught by his first Actions, so, from the Bent of a stubborn Disposition Events could not correct, he took care to inculcate it from time to time, as long as it was in his Power to act at all.

Colonel *Clive* used repeated Endeavours to extricate him, if he would have permitted it, out of all his Difficulties. He laboured in his Letters to convince him, that as the Attack and Reduction of *Chandenagore* proceeded entirely from the Behaviour of the *French* themselves, so it could not be any-way prejudicial to him, or to his Subjects. He assured him, that the *English* would not suffer his Revenue to be impaired, by their being Masters of the Place; but were disposed, under equitable Conditions, to re-place the Customs paid by the *French*; and that they were well satisfied with their own Possessions, and did not desire to enlarge or to extend them. On the contrary, they were ready to give him whatever Satisfaction he could demand, of their Willingness to acquiesce under any Terms, and to comply with such Measures as should appear most expedient for restoring and preserving the Tranquility of his Country; that their Minds were entirely set upon Commerce; that they became military merely by Force; but that they most ardently wished to return to, and be known by him only in, their old Occupation of Merchants; that, as things stood, their Interest rendered it absolutely requisite to expel the *French* out of *Bengal*, to prevent new Disputes, which was his Interest likewise; and that, if he would do it himself, they should be well satisfied, and consider it as a Favour. That he had been exceedingly imposed upon, in respect to the Conduct of that Nation, on the Coast of *Coromandel*, where the *Nabobs* they had espoused were obliged to make exorbitant Grants, in Acknowledgement for their Assistance; that, in consequence of this, they had torn away whole Provinces, of which they were in full Possession; while, on the other hand, the *English* had lent the *Nabobs*, with whom they had taken Part, purely on account of their being the King's Officers, very large Sums of Money; with the Repayment of which they would be well content, without soliciting, extorting, or even accepting any Grants whatever. That he might from thence judge of the Temper of the two Nations and the Difference that he would find in having either of them for his Allies; and that therefore, if he regarded his own Welfare, he would adhere strictly to, and punctually fulfil, the Treaty he had made; which if he did, he might not only rely upon the Support that had been promised him, but that he might be assured, he would personally lose the last Drop of his Blood, and sacrifice the last Man under his Command, in his Service, against any of his real Enemies, whenever his Occasions might require it. Vice-Admiral *Watson* wrote also to him to the same Purpose.

The Suba, who was equally dissatisfied with and disturbed at the State of his Affairs, and found himself obliged to be at a great Expence in keeping Troops in the Field, knew not what to say or how to act. He declared, however, positively, against our reducing the *French* subordinate Factories; would not hear of making the Remains of their Forces Prisoners, and delivering them up to the *English*; but, however, discovered no Scruple at all in seizing upon their Effects, under Colour of doing it to make Satisfaction to his own Subjects, who were their Creditors. At the same time he ordered the *French* to quit his Dominions, directing them to march towards *Patna*. He likewise paid farther Sums of Money to the Company's Servants, and gave them Hopes, that he would both strictly and speedily fulfil his Treaty in every respect. In regard to the Artillery, which he did not restore, he alleged, that he was distressed himself for want of Cannon, and was willing to purchase them. In this manner things went on for a Month or Six Weeks, during which Space every Method was practised that could lessen his Apprehensions, or free him from that Terror which he seemed to have of the *English* advancing their Forces into the Heart of his Country. He was even permitted, upon a Rumour that the Garrison of *Cassimbuzar* was augmented to Five hundred Men, to send his own Officers to inspect it, who found and reported, that there was not above a Tenth Part of the Number. The same Compliances were made in many Respects.

But in the midst of these Compliances and Concessions, instead of growing milder and better disposed, the Suba shewed very evident Marks of his being more and more exasperated against those who gave them. He fell again to caballing with the *French*; and instead of compelling those who had escaped to quit his Country, as he engaged expressly, he took that little Body of Men, which were about *Patna*, into his Pay, at the Rate of Ten thousand Rupees a Month, of which Mr. *Watts* procured the Intelligence, and communicated it to the Committee. He turned all his Attention towards Mr. *Bussy*, who, as he was made to believe, had an Army of Twenty thousand Men, and with which he might march speedily into his Dominions. When these Rumours at any time sunk, he was more tractable; but as soon as they revived, he became as imperious and as much out of Humour as ever. Vice-Admiral *Watson* having sent him Several pressing Letters, exhorting him to act suitable to his Dignity, agreeable to his own Interests, for the Good of his Subjects, to give no Ear to idle Reports, to accomplish his Promises, and fulfil the several Articles of his Treaty, he gave no Answers to them, but complained that they wrote in so severe a Stile, that he knew not how to reply to them. At length his Uneasinesses, Jealousies, and Suspicions, rose so high, that he ordered all the Boats to be searched that came up to *Cassimbuzar*, and publickly declared, that if any Powder or Ammunition was found aboard, that he would order the Noses and Ears of the Watermen to be cut off, which was a direct Breach of his Treaty. He could not help knowing, that this Method of acting must have a very disadvantageous Effect upon the Affairs of the *English* in his Dominions, and impede and perplex their Commercial Transactions exceedingly. He could not be ignorant that this would diminish his own Income, distress his Subjects, and lessen both their Subsistence and their Industry. But alas! he was so much under the Dominion of his Passions, that he considered only gratifying his Caprice; and acting from no Motive, could discern no Consequences. Hapless as a Man! more hapless as a Prince! he had as little Fear of falling into Difficulties, as, when fallen, he had Skill to get out of them.

An Attempt has been already made to give the Reader some Idea of the melancholy and mortifying Situation of Mr. *Watts*, who resided on the Part of the Company at the Suba's Court, whose Perplexities daily increased, and whose Anxieties hourly multiplied, though they had not yet reached to those Circumstances of Disgust and Distress that they afterwards did. He saw himself almost constantly on bad Terms with that Prince, and of course upon no good ones with his Ministers and Favourites. The Suba never forgave him extracting that important, and, as he conceived it, fatal Letter of Permission to Admiral *Watson*; to which, without much Injustice, he ascribed solely the attacking and taking *Chandenagore*. It was from Mr. *Watts* he received, from Day to Day, those grating Remonstrances that so much displeased him, and those admonitory Letters that made still a deeper Impression. He ought, in Strictness, to have considered him, on these Occasions, as the Instrument only of the Company; but his Warmth and Assiduity in all these frequent Applications, made the Suba look no farther than himself. He was obliged to confer with him daily, and, if he was absent, called for him, as being uneasy if he missed him, whence of course he beheld him often, and yet but very seldom with a gracious Eye. Mr. *Watts* saw, felt, and understood these numberless Inconveniencies, to which he was exposed, and which, as we have observed, heightened upon him every Hour. But the Consolation he derived from the kind Letters of Admiral *Watson* and Colonel *Clive*, who had a true and lively Sense of his Services and Sufferings, kept up his Spirits, and enabled him to pursue his Business with a Vivacity that entirely concealed, though it could not remove, but rather augmented, his interior Chagrin. Besides this, he had another Satisfaction, which was getting most Part of the Treaty executed, tho with infinite Trouble; and this procured him the hearty Approbation of the Select Committee, who were now convinced, that he not only did all that could be done, but more than most Men could have done in his Station. As ill as he was treated by him, he continued to render the Suba many good Offices; giving the Committee to understand, that, in all human Probability, they should gradually obtain all that they desired, and that therefore they should not be impatient. He prevailed also upon Colonel *Clive* to promise the Suba from time to time his Assistance; and he laboured more incessantly to convince that Prince, that, if he would confide in the *English*, he had no Reason to fear either foreign or domestic Enemies, with which, when he thought himself in Danger, he was well enough pleased; but when that was in any Degree over, he shewed a visible Uneasiness at his having confessed that he stood in need of such Assistance.

The Storm, that had been gathering from the Beginning of *March*, began to burst about the latter End of *April*, and in the Opening of the Month of *May*; when the Suba, in sudden Starts of Passion, shewed the Rancour of his Heart, and testified sufficiently, that he waited only for an Opportunity to make the *English* feel a second Time the heavy Weight of his Resentment. As he never assigned any Causes himself, but on the contrary, even in this Interval, and in the midst of Actions inconsistent with those Declarations, asserted his Intention to fulfil his Treaty, and appealed to God and his Prophet for the Truth of it; we must own it is extremely difficult to guess at his Reasons. They appear, however, to have been chiefly Three; First, the perpetual Insinuations of the *French*, that Mr. *Bussy* might be brought to his Assistance; and that, by a Junction with his Troops, he would be greatly superior to the *English*; and to this Measure he was so much inclined, that he actually wrote a Letter to that Officer, in which he promised him Twenty Lack of Rupees, if he would march directly into his Dominions, of which Mr. *Watts* also gave the Intelligence. The next Thing was, the Compliances that had been made with a View of gaining him, the recalling most of the Troops from *Chandenagore*, the permitting him to keep the Cannon, to search the Factory of *Cassimbuzar*, and the warm and tender Expressions of Friendship in Colonel *Clive*'s Letters, with the high Testimonies of Reverence and Respect paid him, whenever he was pleased to be in a good Temper, or to profess his Disposition of adhering to his Engagements. The last was, the Retreat of the *Patans*, who had shewn an Intention to invade his Territories, and the putting an End to the Troubles occasioned by the *My Rajah*, by which he thought himself in a Condition to employ all his Forces, and was likewise secure of having the *French* to manage his Artillery, with which they made him believe they could perform Wonders. In these Circumstances he was so very elate, as not to make any Scruple (though a direct Breach of his Faith) of interrupting the *English* Commerce, keeping his Army in the Field, though he had most solemnly promised the contrary, and sometimes expressing a formal Design of sending back the Treaty that had been signed with him, and demanding his own. In such a State of Things it was evident, that the Company could not rely upon him, or consider themselves in any Degree of Security, farther than as they were supported by the King's Squadron and Forces; and as their present Condition was very precarious, so their future Prospect was still more gloomy and alarming; and though as yet they were not in a state of War, they could not, however, with any Propriety, be said to be in Peace.

The Vice-Admiral and Colonel *Clive* were exceedingly embarrassed, and found it very difficult to judge what Measures they were to take. If they advanced their Forces, or resumed their military Preparations, it might, in Appearance, justify the Suba's Behaviour; and besides, Mr. *Watts* and the Select Committee both dissuaded any Steps of this kind, as inconsistent with the Company's Concerns, at least till they had secured the Money and Effects of the several Subordinates. On the other hand, they saw that

Compliances did more Harm than Good, and that their Professions of adhering inviolably to the Peace, and their repeated Promises of Friendship and Assistance, only flattered the Suba's Pride, heightened his Notions of his own Power, and encouraged him to act with greater Violence and Insolence, of which they had but too many, and those flagrant Instances. Colonel *Clive*, however, took on one Side every Method that was necessary to demonstrate his pacific Inclination, and how sincere his Intentions were to restore and preserve the Tranquility of the Provinces, desisting from his Demands that the *French* should be delivered up, from the repairing the Fortifications at *Cassimbuzar*, or reinforcing the Garrison. At the same time, he wrote in very plain Terms to the Suba, told him his Thoughts of his Proceedings, the Concern they gave him, and the Determination he had taken, to recur to open Force, whenever he found, from his Manner of acting, that no other Remedy was left, and that it was entirely in his Power to have him for a Friend or an Enemy. In the very Height of these Disputes, the Suba demanded an ample Acquittance, under the Seal of the Governor and Select Committee, and those also of the Vice-Admiral and Colonel. To this the latter wrote him for Answer, that it was strange he should demand, or expect such an Acquittance, when he very well knew, that several of the Articles were still unperformed; that many Lacks of Rupees were due to the Company, in Satisfaction of their Losses; that the Restitution of Thirty-eight Villages, which they claimed, had not yet been made; and that their Commerce in general was still interrupted. But as his Demand might imply a Resolution to settle all these Points, and as it was hoped this was really the Case, such an Acquittance should be immediately prepared, and transmitted to Mr. *Watts*, with express Orders to deliver it, as soon as the Articles hitherto unadjusted were once thoroughly settled.

This, however reasonable in itself, was by no means acceptable to the Suba, who, in Proportion as he lost all seeming Regard, though really he never had any for the Vice-Admiral and the Colonel, towards both of whom he had once professed so much Esteem, kept no longer any Measures towards Mr. *Watts*, whom he looked upon as a Man he could not deceive, as a Man whom he hated for that Reason, and, which was an additional Motive to his Resentment, though it should, if his Mind had corresponded with his Rank, have restrained it, as a Man absolutely in his Power. In order to execute the various Commissions with which he was charged more punctually, Mr. *Watts*, according to the Custom of *Indostan*, had employed a Person to act as his Agent, in the Language of the Country, a *Vaqueel*. Him, in the first Fit of his Fury, the Suba forbid his Court. An Affront very gross in *India*, though in Appearance, and to us, unacquainted with their Customs, a very slight Thing, but it was quickly followed by personal Insults, and those of the most serious Nature. At last, forgetting the Respect due to the *British* Crown, to Mr. *Watts*'s Character as Resident from the *East India* Company, and his own Dignity, he told several of his principal Ministers, with a View that they should, as they really did, tell it Mr. *Watts* again, that, upon the first Intelligence he had of the Motion of the *English* Troops, he would cut off that Gentleman's Head, or cause him to be impaled. This was such an Outrage on the Law of Nations as was inconsistent with the Rank of a Prince, and must, by the Rules of common Sense, leave any Man in his Circumstances at Liberty to take the Methods that appeared to him safest for his own Preservation. Upon this Occasion Mr. *Watts* acted with a Degree of Temper and Calmness that must surprize the Reader. He wrote an Account of the Facts to the Governor, without any Exaggeration, adding, that he despised the Suba's Threatenings, and desired the Select Committee would proceed as the Company's Interest directed, and without putting themselves in Pain for his Safety. A Circumstance that would not have been inserted in these Memoirs, if the Person was not alive to whom that Letter was addressed.

The Gentlemen entrusted with the Direction of Affairs, saw plainly the Tendency of the Suba's Proceedings. Indeed they were so evident, as to fill all the Inhabitants of *Calcutta* with Alarms, that were but too well founded. Experience had already taught them, how far the Caprice of the Suba might go; and it was no way improbable, that if they were so unhappy as to fall again under his Power, they might, if possible, meet with still worse Treatment, which induced them to make the best Provision they could for their Defence; and to put the Troops into such Condition, as that, whenever Necessity required, they might be able to repel Force by Force. At the same time, however, it was resolved, not to precipitate any thing, to act with the utmost Caution, and to lay hold of any favourable Opportunity that might offer, towards furnishing Means to extricate them from these Perplexities.

Calcutta was not the only Place where Doubts and Apprehensions reigned. They were to the full as strong in *Muxadavad*, with this additional and distinguishing Circumstance, that Discord spread itself through the Suba's Court, where the only Oracle that every Man consulted was his own Interest. Reverses of Fortune were equally sudden and frequent. The Courtiers that were in the highest Favour To-day, were To-morrow in the very Depth of Disgrace. No Man was secure, and therefore no Man was contented; and which is, and will be always the Case in corrupt Courts, the worst Men had the best Chance. Those who had nothing to lose, had all Things to expect; and by flattering their Prince's Humour, and complying blindly with all his Commands, the meanest and basest People about him grew quickly the most considerable. Those who had been in the Old Suba's Councils and Confidence, who were Men of Rank and Family, and who had both Estates and Reputations to risque, were, from those very Circumstances, Malecontents. They saw that this System could not last long; that a general Confusion must ensue; and that a Man, governed entirely by his Passions, could never carry on public Affairs with any Degree of Success. But these Reflections, which their own good Sense and long Experience suggested to them, served only to disturb and to distract, without affording them the least Glance of extricating either him or themselves from that impending Ruin, which his rash and raw Measures rendered inevitable. They perceived plainly enough each other's Sentiments, from that Tincture which they naturally gave to every One's Language and Behaviour; but they had no Confidence at all amongst themselves, and every Man was afraid of hastening his own particular Fall, by disclosing or lamenting the Approach of that common Destruction, which, however visible to their Understandings, was by no means a fit Subject for their Conversation.

But in the midst of these Perplexities a Ray of Hope very unexpectedly appeared. The Suba had shewn the Severity of his Nature, in so many Instances, as to strike a universal Terror; more especially as the Fickleness of his Disposition suffered no Man who was near him, and in his Power, to think himself safe. In such a State of general Danger, there occurred to every One, capable of thinking freely (the only Species of Liberty that even Tyrants' Favourites retain) but one single Mode of Security, which consisted in depriving him of his Power, who so constantly, as well as egregiously abused it. The Conception of this availed little, since the Attempt was equally difficult and dangerous; and the failing in it sure to be attended with sudden and certain Destruction. There was also but one way to move, or rather to lessen the Risk; and this also was very easily discovered. It was procuring the Countenance and the Assistance of the *English*. Such as were in the Suba's Confidence, and from that very Circumstance most afraid of him, were persuaded they could merit very much from the Company's Servants, by laying open his Secrets, and thereby shewing them, what these People thought they did not in the least suspect, the Danger to which they stood exposed. Amongst several who reasoned thus in their own Breasts, there was one who had a considerable share of Interest and Authority. His Name was *Godar Yar Cawn Laitty*, who, when he had for some time meditated, and in his own Mind thoroughly digested his Scheme, thought it wore so fair an Appearance, that he sent several Messages to Mr. *Watts*, signifying that he had something to communicate to him of great Importance: But the Suba kept so many Spies upon that Gentleman, and those Spies watched him so very closely, that it was simply impossible to comply with *Godar Yar Cawn Laitty*'s Request of having an Interview with him, because it was evidently risking the utter Ruin of both. Some Days, therefore, elapsed, before an Expedient could be found to remove this troublesome Obstacle, and to give Mr. *Watts* the necessary Information of what were this Person's real Intentions, and what the Means by which he proposed to carry them into Execution.

He at length thought proper to send to him *Omichund*, who has been mentioned before, in order to draw what Lights he could from this discontented Confident of the Suba, who, after he had conferred with him, reported, that he knew with Certainty his Master's settled Intentions were to break with and to attack the *English*, as soon as he had a favourable Opportunity; that he likewise knew the Suba had retained the *French*, who had escaped from *Chandenagore*, and in the subordinate Factories, in his Service, who were to remain at *Patna* in his Pay, till an Occasion could be found for employing them; that the *English* had no Method of preventing this threatening Tempest from breaking upon their Establishments, but by providing in Time a Force sufficient to resist it; that he was willing, whenever the Suba should recur to open Hostilities, to join Us, and act against him, provided we would assist him in assuming the Government of the Province; that in return for this, he would, as soon as he was fixed in that Office, grant, by way of Recompence, a large Extent of Lands to the Company, and would likewise pay down a Sum in ready Money, sufficient to indemnify the People of *Calcutta* for all the Losses they had sustained. These were Communications of so dangerous as well as so delicate a Nature, that they would infallibly have turned a weak Head, or distracted a timid Mind. They were received calmly and coolly, as Points of Information, in regard to which Mr. *Watts* could take no Step of himself, but from which the Persons who had communicated them had nothing to fear; and with these Assurances, such was their Opinion of his Secrecy, Sagacity, and Steadiness, that they remained perfectly satisfied and easy, leaving him sufficient Leisure to consider and reflect upon these very extraordinary Overtures, and to review and digest the Thoughts that must naturally arise upon so important a Subject. But, however, restrained him within the Compass of Six Days, to procure for this *Moorish* Officer an Answer, from those who were entrusted with the Management of the Company's Affairs at *Calcutta.*

The Situation of Mr. *Watts* in this Conjuncture, is much more easy to conceive than to describe. He was oppressed with Cares, environed with Perils, and had not so much as a single Person with whom to communicate or to consult. His own Safety, the Welfare, and even the Being of the *British* Settlements, and indeed the future Fate of these Provinces, depended, at least in the first Instance, on his Capacity, Penetration, and Discretion. It was a very arduous Task to form any clear Opinion upon this Offer; it demanded much Skill to set the Motives upon which such an Opinion must be founded in their proper Light; and, when all this was done, it appeared infinitely hazardous to transmit Propositions of this Nature, together with his Thoughts upon them, to *Calcutta*, while a jealous Prince, in a Country where the Character of a Spy is not dishonourable, had Multitudes of such

State Implements about him, all filled with the Hopes of rising upon his Ruin. But though perfectly sensible of all this, as he must have been to counteract their Vigilance, he boldly undertook, and as happily performed, all that the Confidence reposed in him, or his Duty to the Company could demand. He stated fully the Nature of these Overtures, the Suba's Disposition at the Time, the Characters and Credit of the principal Officers about him, their Tempers, Circumstances, and Connections, the Probability that such a Design might be carried into Execution, the Hazards to which it must be exposed, and the Methods most proper to avoid them. But when he had done all this, he added no direct Judgment of his own. He contented himself with giving Lights, without venturing to pronounce what Measure ought to be taken. He had frequent Experience of the Regard paid by them to his Sentiments, from his having commonly sent them the Draughts of the Letters to the Suba, which being transmitted back to him, he presented to that Prince; but he held this to be a Matter too difficult, as well as too delicate for him to determine. He knew very well there was no small Danger in Delay; but he likewise knew, that there was still more Danger in a rash Decision, and therefore he gave none. The Select Committee concurred with him in this; they entertained the Motion, commended his Caution, suggested that he should continue to keep Things in Suspense, but directed him by all Means to avoid concluding any Thing, till he should receive their future Directions in a Thing of so great Weight.

It was not long after this, that *Meer Jaffeir Aly Cawn*, a Person of great Distinction, who had married the Sister of *Aliverdy Cawn*, the Suba's Grandfather and Predecessor, sent one in whom he could perfectly confide to Mr. *Watts*, to disclose what were his real Opinions, and how very short a Space he thought was like to intervene, before the Suba took the Field once more, against the *English*. This Person had it farther in Commission to represent, that the Disaffection of the principal Officers, Civil and Military, was in a manner general; that *Meer Jaffeir* never appeared in the Suba's Presence, without Fear of being assassinated; and that for this Reason, whenever he was constrained to go, he always caused his Forces to be drawn out, under Arms, with his Son at their Head. In the Close of his Discourse, he added, that a Determination was already taken, to depose, for their own Sakes, *Suraja Dowlat*; and that if the *English* would engage with, and promise to support, another Person, in assuming the Dignity of Suba, *Rahim Cawn, Roydoolub*, and *Bahadar Aly Cawn*, were ready to join *Meer Jaffeir*, in removing *Suraja Dowlat*, whose Affairs would be then in a very desperate Situation. Mr. *Watts* transmitted the Detail of this Conversation also to Colonel *Clive*, and gave it as his own Opinion, that *Meer Jaffeir* was by far the properest Person to be elevated to that Rank, as his Abilities were greater, his Reputation better, and his Connections more extensive than those of *Laitty*. He at the same time acquainted the Colonel, that if this Change was to be accomplished by their Forces, as he much doubted, whether, after all, the *Moors* had Spirit enough to attempt so extraordinary an Enterprize themselves, it would be right to form the Outlines of a new Agreement, of which the old one ought to be the Basis; and to frame such additional Articles, as might effectually indemnify the Company for the Risk they ran, and procure an ample Satisfaction for the Losses private Persons had sustained, in the Devastation of *Calcutta*, of which no Care had been taken in the former Treaty; and that, in short, nothing should now be omitted, that might put their Affairs for the future upon a firm and stable Establishment; so that, in case of Disturbances in the Country, the Servants of the Company, and those who depended on it, might be in a Condition to protect themselves.

As these Transactions were of a very delicate Nature, and were to be conducted with much Discretion, and of course with some Delay, the Suba had a Season of Recess, in which, by a Change of Measures, he might have recovered his Authority, have resettled his distracted Government, and repaired all his past Errors. He not only neglected this entirely, but continued acting, in every respect, as if he had aimed at his own Destruction. He endeavoured to negotiate Succours from some of his Neighbours, who, though they knew not the Weakness of his Condition, and therefore civilly entertained his Proposals, had however such an Opinion of the Weakness of his Conduct, that nothing could induce them to enter into his Measures. He continued corresponding with Mr. *Bussy*, from whom he received Letters, which served to support and increase his Delusion, and to flatter him with the Hopes of seeing an Army of Twenty thousand Men in his

Dominions, which, could he have brought them, would have tended only to have impoverished his Subjects, and to have given him new Masters, under the Title of old Allies. He was courted all this time by Colonel *Clive* to lay down his Arms, to settle the few remaining unaccomplished Articles in the Treaty, and, above all, to put the Trade of his Territories into its usual Channel, for the common Benefit of the *Europeans* and the Natives. To these Solicitations he gave no Answers, or such as afforded no sort of Satisfaction; but, on the contrary, indicated very plainly, by every Step he took, that he meditated new Disturbances, and waited for what should appear to him a favourable Occasion for renewing the War. In reference, on the other hand, to his own People, he grew every Day more and more intolerable, removing, disgracing, insulting, those whom he had formerly treated with the greatest Marks of Favour and Respect, and of whom several fled privately and in Disguise to seek Shelter in the *English* Territories, and particularly in that of *Cassimbuzar*. By this Behaviour he not only augmented the Disaffection that had already spread so far amongst his Servants, but likewise furnished so many and such authentic Proofs of his having still the same Points in View, that he had at his Entrance on the Administration, and of the Obstinacy of his Aversion to the *English*, so contrary to the Mutability of his Temper in every thing else, that it contributed exceedingly to fortify the Sentiments of those, who maintained, that the Peace of that Part of *India* could never be effectually restored, so long as he held the Supreme Power.

After the Propositions made by Mr. *Watts* had been duly canvassed, and their Importance maturely considered, by the Select Committee, who upon this Occasion framed and took an Oath of Secrecy, they were unanimously approved, and the Project or Draught of a new Treaty was transmitted to him. But at the same time there was great Latitude left, in case of Objections; and he was requested to procure as many and as large Concessions as might be, in case he found it impracticable to obtain every one of the Conditions in the full Extent that they desired. Indeed they relied so entirely upon him, that a Blank was left for the Company's Demand in their Draught of the Treaty for him to fill up; and how it was filled up, will appear from the Treaty itself. This was not only expedient but necessary, as he was upon the Spot, knew the Persons with whom he was treating, their Connections and

Circumstances, and the Motives which might render any of these Demands agreeable or disagreeable. The use Mr. *Watts* made of this Confidence was such as it deserved, and turned not a little to the Advantage of those who gave it. He was himself perfectly sensible, and took all imaginable Pains to make those he dealt with no less sensible, that, notwithstanding this Change was for their mutual Benefit, yet the Weight, the Hazard, and the Expence, would fall principally at least, very probably wholly, upon the *English*. He represented, therefore, effectually, that for such extraordinary Assistance, which alone could put the Means of making it into their Power, a proper Satisfaction ought in Justice to be made, and that this suitable Satisfaction should be made likewise in a proper Manner. He was apprehensive also, upon this Head, that a false Delicacy might produce future Disputes, and therefore very prudently provided, that the unliquidated Demands in the Sketch should be reduced to a Certainty. He also enlarged the Sums stipulated for the Losses of private Persons, and distinguished them under National Heads; that, if possible, no Jealousies or Heart-burnings might arise in the Colony, when they came to be actually paid.

The surest as well as the shortest Method of setting this Matter in a true Light, and that will at once place it in the strongest, is to insert the original Plan of the new Alliance, as transmitted to Mr. *Watts*, and then the Project settled by that Gentleman, which the Reader will hereafter have an Opportunity of comparing with the Alliance concluded.

Copy of the ARTICLES of Agreement
sent by Colonel *Clive* to *William Watts*, Esq; *May* 2, 1757.

AN Alliance offensive and defensive against all Enemies: The *French* Fugitives to be taken and delivered up to us; all their Factories to be delivered up to us, in order to be destroyed; the *French* never to be permitted to re-settle in this Subaship; in Consideration of which, the *English* Company will annually pay the Amount of Duties usually paid into the King's Treasury on the *French* Trade, or a Sum not exceeding Fifty thousand Rupees annually.

Restitution of the Company's Loss, by the taking of *Calcutta*, and their Out Settlements; also Restitution for the Losses of all *Europeans* by *Ditto*, as may be stated fairly by Admiral *Watson*, the Governor, Colonel *Clive*, *William Watts*, Esq; Major *Kilpatrick*, and Mr. *Becher*.

Blacks and *Armenians* are not included.

That the whole of our Phirmaund be complied with, and all other Grants made to us, particularly in the Treaty with *Suraja Dowlat*.

That the Bounds of *Calcutta* are to extend the whole Circle of *Ditchdug*, upon the Invasion of the *Marattes*; also Six hundred Yards without it, for an Esplanade.

The Inhabitants within our Bounds to be entirely subject to the *English* Laws and Government.

That we have Liberty to fortify and garrison our Factories of *Cassimbuzar* and *Dacca*, as we think proper, and a sufficient Esplanade be granted us round each.

That Convoys to and from one of our Settlements to another, be permitted to pass without Interruption or Molestation.

That the *Moors* shall erect no Fortifications within Twenty Miles of the River Side, from *Hughley* to *Ingelee*.

That a Tract of Land be made over to the *English* Company, whose Revenues shall be sufficient to maintain a proper Force of *Europeans* and Seapoys, to keep out the *French*, and assist the Government against all Enemies.

That whenever the *English* Troops are called to the assistance of the Government, that the extraordinary Expences of the Campaign be made good by the Government.

That an *English* Gentleman, in Quality of Envoy, be permitted to reside at Court, and be treated with due Respect.

Minutes of the Treaty, by Mr. *Watts, May 14, 1757.*

I.   That he will confirm all the Grants the former Nabob made us.

II.   He will make an Alliance with the *English*, offensive and defensive, against all Enemies, either Natives or *Europeans*

III.   Whatever *French* are in his Provinces of *Bengal, Bahar*, or *Orixa*, to be delivered up with all their Houses and Factories, and they never permitted to settle more in either of those Provinces.

IV.   On Account of the Company's Loss[1]   1   Crore.

V.   On Account of the Losses of *Europeans*   30   Lack.

VI.   On Account of the Losses of *Jentoows*   30   Lack.

VII.   On Account of the Losses of *Armenians*   10   Lack.

VIII.   On Account of the Losses for *Omichund*   30   Lack.

IX.   Whatever Ground there is within the *Calcutta* Ditch, belonging to the *Zemindars*, to be given to the *English*, and Six hundred Yards without the Ditch all round.

X.   A Tract of Land, whose Rents in the King's Books amounts to 100,000 Rupees Yearly, to be bought at a reasonable Value, from the Zemindary, and the Nabob to assist us in the Purchase, we paying the annual Piscash or Revenue, as usual, to the Nabob. Whatever Profit may arise from this Zemindary, is to go towards paying our Military.

---

[1] The Rupee is a Silver Coin, struck in the *Moghul*'s Mints, with an Inscription of his Name and Titles, the Year of his Reign, and the Place at which it was struck. It weighs from 7 *dw.* 10⅓ *gr.* to 7 *dw.* 11 *gr.* and the Proportion of Allay to fine Silver, is as 1 or 2 to 100. One hundred thousand Rupees make a Lack, One hundred Lacks a Coroe or Crore, One hundred Crores an Arrib.

XI. Whenever the Nabob wants the Assistance of our Troops, the extraordinary Expence to be paid by him.

His Plan of the Treaty was returned, with Alterations: Some of the Articles were modified, and a Blank left for the Company's Demand, that in case *Meer Jaffeir* should think it too extravagant, Mr. *Watts* might have Liberty to moderate it, and he was desired to get it carried into Execution; but it will appear in the Treaty itself, which will be hereafter given, that Mr. *Watts* got the Treaty executed, without any Deduction or Modification. This was a Work equally arduous and hazardous, as Things then stood, when every Look, every Word, every Motion of his was suspected, and which at the same time rendered the procuring its Conclusion expeditiously a Circumstance of the utmost Consequence. In all this, the Risk might be truly said to fall entirely upon himself; so that it is not easy to imagine, how any Man's Circumstances could be more critical than his actually were in this Conjuncture. We shall however see, that they really became so afterwards, and this in a very high Degree, and in very many Respects, from Causes that could not be avoided, and which produced a Train of unforeseen Events.

It was pretty early known, that *Meer Jaffeir* had entertained no very favourable Notion of *Omichund*, but there was a Necessity of employing and trusting him notwithstanding, of which though the former did not

TABLE of RUPEES.

Lack of Rupees.	£. *Sterling.*
1	12,500
10	125,000
20	250,000
30	375,000
40	500,000
50	625,000
60	750,000
70	875,000
80	1,000,000
90	1,125,000
A Crore	1,250,000

complain, yet he did not dislike him the less. In the midst of these arduous Transactions, and when every one else had their Hands and their Hearts full, it came into *Omichund*'s Head to practise a little upon *Suraja Dowlat*, probably that he might be sure of somewhat, however Things went. He mentioned to Mr. *Watts* this very fine-spun Project, to which, that it appeared wild and strange, was by no means the strongest Objection. It was, however, in vain to make any: there was Money he thought to be got, and, if it was possible, he was resolved to get it. On the Sixteenth of *May* he went to the Palace, where, exerting his admirable Faculty of magnifying the Utility and exalting the Credit of the Advice he had to give, and having first alarmed the Suba's timid Mind, by touching many Subjects he knew were disagreeable, and in the Close, when he saw him sufficiently amazed, condescended to hint, that he had found means, with great Difficulty, to come at a Secret of the last Consequence, and for the revealing of which he was sure to lose his Life, if it was so much as suspected that he had penetrated and disclosed it. Promises of every kind were made, and at length out it came, that the *English* had discovered all his Negotiations with Mr. *Bussy*, some Circumstances of which he mentioned; that, upon this, they had sent two Gentlemen to confer with, and to convince him, how much more it would be for his Interest to concur with them; and that they had made, or were upon the Point of making, a Peace; which, without doubt, must be at his Expence. As strange as it may seem, *Omichund* prevailed over a Man's Foibles, which he had studied, and deluded him into a firm Belief of all he said, and, in consequence of this, he procured a Perwannah, that is, an Order from the Suba to the Burdwan Rajah, one of his Officers, for the Payment of Four Lack of Rupees which he owed him, and the full Restitution of the remaining Part of the Money, and all the Goods, of which he had been despoiled at *Calcutta*. This he took wonderful Care to have immediately executed, for fear of Accidents, that very Night; neither did he remain within the Suba's Reach long after. He left Traces, however, behind him, that sufficiently justified *Meer Jaffeir*'s Suspicions, and exerted that Power of perplexing, which he possessed in full as eminent a Degree as that of persuading. This was one principal Cause of those new Difficulties, to which Mr. *Watts* found himself exposed, when he thought the whole Stock of his Abilities small enough to deal with the old ones.

When the Agreement came to be offered to *Roydoolub*, one of the Suba's principal Ministers, but, notwithstanding that, one of the Parties to this Treaty, he made a Doubt as to the Possibility of complying with it. He said, the Treasury, since the Death of the Old Suba, *Aliverdy Cawn*, had been much drained, and that though *Suraja Dowlat* was indeed very rapacious, yet he managed his Affairs so ill, by keeping his Forces so long in the Field, as to have impoverished himself by a vast, and at the same time useless Expence. He also suggested, that possibly in the Confusion that commonly attends every Revolution, the Suba's Treasury might be plundered, and then they should remain bound, without having it in their Power to pay. But to remove these Difficulties, he proposed it as an Expedient, to divide whatever was found in the Treasury with the *English*. Mr. *Watts*, who understood these People perfectly, consented to sign the Treaty with such a Clause, subject to the Approbation of the Select Committee at *Calcutta*. But when *Roydoolub* reflected, that upon such a Division he could pretend to no Commission, as he might on Money issued in virtue of the Treaty, of which he had Hopes given him; when Things came to a Crisis, he relinquished his own Proposal, and resolved to sign the Treaty as it stood. It appeared, that the Apprehensions which occasioned these Disputes, and this Delay, were infused into *Roydoolub* by *Omichund*, who gave him to understand, that if once the *English* Army took Possession of *Muxadavad*, they would not leave it again in three Years. This old crafty Man was not satisfied with giving this Proof of his Skill in embarrassing; he went much farther; and as soon as he was himself out of Danger, divulged the Secret, which brought Mr. *Watts*, as well as *Meer Jaffeir* and the rest, to the very Brink of Destruction; while at *Calcutta* he represented the whole Design as become desperate and impracticable, because it was discovered. It was, indeed, wonderful, all Things, and more especially his Behaviour, considered, that it was not so. However, this Effect these Rumours had, that Confusion increased, Discontent spread itself more and more in the Suba's Camp, and the Divisions between him and his principal Officers grew daily wider and wider. *Meer Jaffeir* was fallen into open Disgrace, removed from his Office of Buxy, or Paymaster; upon which he withdrew, and continued in his Quarters with his Troops, and came no more near the Suba. A Circumstance that rendered it next to impossible for Mr. *Watts*, who was sensible that he had many Spies upon his Conduct, to have an Interview with him, whose House was entirely surrounded by the Nabob's Forces, without its being known; and this had given the Suba an Opportunity of executing his Threats, and if that had been a Thing he regarded, without much injuring his Reputation. The Matter, though so much embarrassed, being still absolutely necessary, and the time pressing, Mr. *Watts* went to him, in a covered Dooley, the Manner in which Women are conveyed in that Country, by which means he escaped Notice, and saw the Treaty which had been signed, sealed, and sworn to on the Koran, and upon his Son's Head, by *Meer Jaffeir*, with all the Solemnity imaginable, in the Evening of the Fifth of *June*. When this was once done, and authentic Advice received of its being done at *Calcutta*, it removed all Surmises, silenced every Suspicion, and by giving entire Satisfaction, made way for the taking those Measures which were requisite for carrying it into Execution.

But before we proceed farther, it will be proper to look upon this Treaty, which with such indefatigable Diligence Mr. *Watts* planned, prosecuted, and brought to bear, in despite of the Suspicions, Spies, and insidious Contrivances, of all his Enemies; by which the Company's Commerce, and all their Establishments in this Part of *India*, were secured, the Losses which the Inhabitants of those Places had sustained, repaired, and the Honour of the Nation vindicated.

Translation of the TREATY made with *Meer Jaffeir*.

Wrote with his own Hand.

I Swear by God, and by the Prophet of God, to abide by the Terms of this Treaty, as long as I have Life.

Mir JAFFEIR KHAN BAHADAR,
Servant of King ALLUMGEER.

TREATY made with the Admiral, Colonel *Clive*, and the other Counsellors, Mr. *Drake* and Mr. *Watts*.

I. *WHATEVER* Articles were agreed upon in the time of Peace with the Nabob, *Suraja Dowlat, Munsurah Mimalek Shaik Kouli Khan Bahadar*, and *Hybut Jung*, I agree to comply with.

II. The Enemies of the *English* are my Enemies, whether they be *Indians* or *Europeans*.

III. All the Effects and Factories belonging to the *French*, in the Provinces of *Bengal, Bahar*, and *Orixa*, shall remain in the Possession of the *English*; nor will I ever allow them to settle any more in the Three Provinces.

IV. In Consideration of the Losses which the *English* Company have sustained, by the Capture and Plunder of *Calcutta*, by the Nabob, and the Charges occasioned by the Maintenance of their Forces, I give them One Coroe of Rupees.

V. For the Effects plundered from the *English* Inhabitants of *Calcutta*, I agree to give them Fifty Lack of Rupees.

VI. For the Effects plundered from the *Gentoows, Mussulmen*, and other Subjects of *Calcutta*, Twenty Lack of Rupees shall be given.

VII. For the Effects plundered from the *Armenian* Inhabitants of *Calcutta*, I will give the Sum of Seven Lack of Rupees. The Distribution to be made of the Sums allotted the Natives, *English* Inhabitants, *Gentoows*, and *Mussulmen*, shall be left to the Admiral, Colonel *Clive, Roger Drake, William Watts, James Kilpatrick*, and *Richard Becher*, Esqrs. to be disposed of by them, to whom they think proper.

VIII. Within the Ditch, which surrounds the Borders of *Calcutta*, are Tracts of Lands belonging to several *Zemindars*, besides which, I will grant to the *English* Company Six hundred Yards without the Ditch.

IX. All the Lands lying to the South of *Calcutta*, as far as *Culpee*, shall be under the Zemindary of the *English* Company, and all the Officers of those Parts shall be under their Jurisdiction; the Revenues to be paid by them in the same Manner with other Zemindars.

X. Whenever I demand the Assistance of the *English*, I will be at the Charge of the Maintenance of their Troops.

XI. I will not erect any new Fortifications near the River *Ganges*, below *Hughley*.

XII. As soon as I am established in the three Provinces, the Sums as aforesaid shall be faithfully paid.

> Dated the 15th *Ramzan*, in the
> Fourth Year of the present Reign.

The perfect Harmony that subsisted between Vice-Admiral *Watson* and Colonel *Clive*, and the intire Confidence reposed in them by the Select Committee, was upon this Occasion, as it had been often before, the principal Source of that Alacrity, with which every thing was undertaken. A Train was immediately provided, a Detachment of Fifty Sailors, with a full Compliment of Officers, appointed to assist those who had the Direction of it; and Instructions were given for stationing a Twenty Gun Ship above *Hughley*, to keep the Communication with the Army open. These Steps were absolutely requisite, and others of a like Nature were prudently contrived, and chearfully performed, by the Officers in the King's and in the Company's Service; the Select Committee did their Business in Silence; and though there was a warm Spirit of Emulation, yet the least Spark of Envy or Jealousy never appeared, though so many Corps of different Kinds were serving conjunctly in the Expedition. This, as it was truly singular, was also remarkably happy; for no Exploit of this Consequence was ever begun or prosecuted in a more critical Situation, or where any untoward Accident might have more easily occasioned a Disappointment. The Forces that were to be employed, tho more numerous than in the preceding Operations, yet were but a Handful, in comparison of the Suba's Army. *Meer Jaffeir*, who had separated his Corps of Troops, was again joined with the Suba, but without any real Reconciliation on either Part: Yet this, however, was sufficient to raise a Doubt, how far any Dependance could be formed upon his acting; and what followed, plainly shewed that Suspicion was not ill founded. There was no small Danger of being surrounded by these superior Troops, and if the Communication with the River had been intercepted, the greatest Difficulties might have ensued. Besides these, the rainy Season was just coming on; so that, all Things taken together, and the Hazard that was to be run being maturely weighed, the *Moors* embarked in this Design had not the smallest Reason to repine at the Price they paid for our Assistance; as on the other hand, their own Safety, and the large Stake for which they fought, being considered, the *English* had great Encouragement to exert themselves with that steady Intrepidity which they did. Mr. *Watts*, from what he knew of the Suba's natural Disposition, and what he had observed with respect to his Forces, and those who commanded them, formed so true a Judgment of all that might happen, and had previously acquainted the Select Committee with these Sentiments, that there scarce fell out any Thing in the Progress of this Expedition which was not foreseen, and in regard to which therefore the proper Precautions had not been taken.

After finishing his Negotiations with *Meer Jaffeir*, and taking all the Measures requisite for executing his intended declining from the Suba in time of Action, and, if a favourable Opportunity offered, seizing his Person, there seemed to be no farther Necessity for Mr. *Watts* to continue under the Eye of a provoked and capricious Prince. But this very Circumstance rendered it expedient; to distract his Thoughts, to give him a Diffidence of the Informations he received, and to afford Leisure for the Preparations making at *Calcutta*. His House was surrounded with Spies, who watched not only his Motions, but his Words and Looks. It may be, the strong Assurances they gave, that he could take no Method to withdraw, but they must have previous Intelligence, contributed to his Safety. However, his Condition was most unhappy; a sudden start of Passion in the Suba had in a Moment brought him to a violent Death, at least; perhaps, to Tortures. At *Calcutta* they had so true a Sense of his Danger, that it was more than once reported, *Suraja Dowlat* had cut off his Head, and set it upon a Pole. There was likewise Doubts as to the Means of his escaping. He chose to do it with the rest of the Gentlemen on Horseback, the Manner least suspected, because of the Length of the Journey, and the extreme Heat of the Season, which rendered it excessively fatiguing, and not a little dangerous. But when he understood from Colonel *Clive*, that every thing respecting the Expedition was completed, he happily deceived the Spies of the Suba, and on the Eleventh of *June* made his Escape, though not unpursued. It was not to *Calcutta* he directed his Course, but to the Army, in which he continued, and was present at the decisive Action which brought on the Completion of his Treaty, and thereby restored Peace to *Bengal*. Let us now resume the Operations of the *British* Forces.

All things being in Readiness, the Army, which consisted of One thousand *Europeans*, Two thousand Seapoys, Fifty Seamen, under the Command of a Lieutenant, with Seven Midshipmen, and Eight Pieces of Cannon, began their March from *Chandenagore* towards *Cassimbuzar* on the 13th of *June*. The very same Day Mr. *Watts* joined the Colonel, to whom he imparted all the Lights, and gave the best Intelligence in every Respect that was in his Power. On the Nineteenth the Town and Fort of *Cutwa*, situated on the same Side with *Chandenagore*, of that River which forms the Island of *Cassimbuzar*, was attacked and taken. This was an Event of some Importance, as it opened a free Passage, which could not have been easily forced, if it had been properly defended. The Army halted there for two Days, in order to receive some Accounts of the Enemies Strength, as well as to gain certain Advice of what might be expected from those who were entered into the Party with, and engaged to support, *Meer Jaffeir*; which, when it arrived, was far enough from being satisfactory or explicit. The Colonel, however, was so well informed by Mr. *Watts*, as to the real Causes of this seeming Backwardness, and had from his own Experience and Penetration so just a Notion of the *Moors* Mode of acting, which, without such previous Acquaintance with their Temper and Manners, might probably have confounded any other Officer in his Station, that on the Twenty-second of the same Month he passed the River, and continued his March directly towards *Plaissy*, where the Army arrived, and took up their Ground about One the next Morning, without meeting with any Disturbance or Molestation on their March.

This Post was extremely well chosen for that Country, and for the Method in which those People make War. It was a Grove, covered on every Side by Mud Banks, in the midst of a Plain. At Day-break, on the Twenty-third, the Suba's Army advanced within a very small Distance, and with a manifest Design to attack the *English* Forces. He had about Fifteen thousand Horse, and between Twenty and Thirty thousand Foot, with upwards of Forty Pieces of heavy Cannon, which were managed by *Frenchmen*, upon whose Skill and Courage he greatly depended. The Van was commanded by *Roydoolub*, and the left Wing by *Meer Jaffeir*. About Six they began to cannonade pretty smartly on every Side, and this Distribution of their Cannon gave them two great Advantages; First, as they were much larger, and carried a heavier Weight of Metal, they did Execution where the *English* Artillery was of no Use; and in the next Place, being thus separated to a considerable Distance from each other, it was impossible to make any Attempt to seize them, and therefore all the Colonel could do was to take the Benefit of his intrenched Posts, and leave his Troops as little exposed as possible. If the Suba, or any of his Officers, had understood well what they were about, they might certainly have prosecuted their Scheme, and have completely invested the *English* Army, and then the Colonel must have waited the Approach of Night, in order to have forced a Passage through the Camp, which he in reality had designed. But the Enemy, on the contrary, upon the falling of a smart Shower about Noon, withdrew their Artillery within their Camp. Upon this, a Detachment marched with Two Field Pieces, and took Possession of a Tank, covered with high Banks, from whence the *Moors* had fired with Success. They then would have brought out their Artillery again, but were prevented; and this encouraged the sending Detachments to possess two other Eminences, very near an Angle of their Camp, covered by a double Breastwork; and from thence, as well as from another Eminence, which still remained in their Possession, they kept up a pretty smart Fire with their Small Arms. They several times endeavoured to bring up Cannon to those Posts, but our Field Pieces were so happily posted, and so well served, that they could never effect it. At length the *English* stormed that Angle and Eminence at the same Instant of time, though the former was defended by Forty *French*, and a very numerous Body of the Suba's Troops, who had likewise in that Post Two Pieces of Cannon, and the latter by a considerable Corps of Foot and Horse. Some Persons of Distinction being killed immediately before, or at the Beginning of the Attack, the Enemy being dispirited by that, quickly gave way, and both the Posts were forced with a very trifling Expence to us, though they suffered severely. On this the right Wing and Center fled, abandoning their Camp and Artillery. Their Loss in this Action fell little, if at all, short of Five hundred Men, and between Forty and Fifty Pieces of Cannon. Of the *English* Forces, there were Twenty killed and Fifty wounded, the greatest Part of which were Seapoys. The Flight of the Enemy was so precipitate, that the Suba, mounted on a Camel, with the better Part of the Army, arrived at *Muxadavad*, which was Twenty Miles distant, by Twelve at Night. The Colonel, after pursuing them Five or Six Miles, halted his Troops, and disposed of them in the best Manner he could. Such was the Battle, such the decisive Victory of *Plaissy*!

It was observed during the Action, that a great Body of Horse, in the Enemy's left Wing, kept mostly hovering at a Distance. But as they made no Signals, though they sometimes advanced within Cannon-shot, they were more than once taught by our Artillery to retire. However, after the Victory was declared, the Colonel was informed that these were *Meer Jaffeir*'s Troops, which remained on the Field in a Body, and the next Day, in the Morning, he had an Interview with Mr. *Clive*, in which, after congratulating him upon his Victory, and applauding his Conduct, he signified his Willingness to ratify the Treaty, and to perform all the Articles of it punctually, as soon as it was in his Power. Colonel *Clive* advised him to march without Delay, and make himself Master of the Capital of the Provinces, before *Suraja Dowlat* could have Time to recollect himself, or draw together any considerable Part of his dispersed Army. *Meer Jaffeir* saw the Utility of this Advice, which he carried into Execution with the utmost

Expedition. At his Entrance into *Muxadavad*, he found the City in the utmost Consternation. The Suba was in Possession of his Palace, on the other Side of the River, with some Troops about him, amongst whom he distributed several Lack of Rupees; but the rest, as had been foreseen, dispersed. A few Hours after, in a Fit of Despair, he withdrew, accompanied only by Five Persons, and took with him a large Sum in Gold, and Jewels to an immense Value. Upon the News of this, *Meer Jaffeir* immediately passed the River, entered the Palace, and assumed the Title of Suba, without any Opposition. At the same time, he seized the Treasures of his Predecessor; and Things being in this Situation, he dispatched Advice instantly to Colonel *Clive*. As there was still a great Fermentation amongst the People, and no Certainty of what was become of *Suraja Dowlat*, it was judged expedient, upon the Arrival of this News, to send Mr. *Watts* and Mr. *Walsh* thither, that they might use their best Endeavours to quiet the Metropolis, to fortify the new Suba, in his Disposition to fulfil the Agreement, and to put an End to the present Confusions, as soon as it was possible. They were fortunate enough to succeed in this important Commission; and all things being reduced to a greater Degree of Order and Tranquility than could well be expected, Colonel *Clive* was invited to pay a Visit to the Nabob. On the Twenty-ninth of *June* he made his public Entry into *Muxadavad*, attended by a Guard of Two hundred *Europeans*, and Three hundred Seapoys. He was received there with the utmost Expressions of Joy, and the loudest Acclamations of the People, as well as with the most profound Marks of Respect, and the warmed Testimonies of Gratitude, by *Meer Jaffeir*, with whom he went to the Palace, and saw him seated in Form, upon the MUSNUD, or Carpet of State, where he was unanimously saluted Suba, and thereby invested with the supreme Authority over the Provinces, with general Applause. Thus, in a Fortnight's Time, this amazing Revolution was begun and ended, and that happy Change effected, from which such numerous Benefits have since flowed to the *East India* Company, and the *British* Subjects in *Bengal*.

About the same time the unfortunate *Suraja Dowlat* was seized, near *Rajamaal*: It is certain that he was in a very low and distressed Condition, with hardly any Cloaths upon his Back, and the Report went, that he sought Shelter in the House of a Man, whose Ears he had caused to be cut off in one of his Transports of Passion, and by whom he was discovered, and given up to his Pursuers. Be that as it will, the making him Prisoner was regarded as an Event of great Consequence to the new Suba. He was no sooner informed of it, than he committed that Prince to the Custody of his Son, recommending to him earnestly in public, to take the surest Methods to prevent his Escape; but at all Events to preserve his Life. The young Man, instead of paying that Respect which was due to his Father's Commands, no sooner had him in his Hands, than he caused him to be privately put to Death. At this, when the Suba appeared to be displeased, his Son alleged, that the captive Suba had found means to write and convey Letters upon the Road to several *Jemidars*, in order excite a Revolt in the Army; to prevent which, he knew no other certain Remedy than that of depriving him of Life, which he thought was likewise better done, without expecting any farther Orders. It has been surmised, and very probably not altogether without Grounds, that there was something of Collusion in this Matter between the Father and the Son; a thing indeed not at all unfrequent in this Part of the World; and what made it pass for a kind of Justice, was the Remembrance that People had, that this unhappy young Man, *Suraja Dowlat*, had been often employed in the very same Acts, by the old Suba, *Aliverdy Cawn*, who availing himself of the sanguinary Disposition of his Grandson, made use of him to remove such as through Avarice, Suspicion, or Resentment, he inclined to have taken away, and then, to save Appearances, disavowed the Fact.

Such was the End of *Suraja Dowlat*, in the Prime of his Youth, being at the Hour of his Death scarce Twenty-five Years of Age. An End! suitable to his Life, which had been spent in Violence and Blood. He was naturally rash and headstrong, conceived the strongest Resentment on the slightest Occasions, often without any Occasion at all; and notwithstanding the Variableness of his Nature, and the continual Fluctuation of his Mind, either executed suddenly the Dictates of his Passion, or, where that was impracticable, persisted in his bad Intentions, though he never shewed any Steadiness in the Performance of his Promises, or any Regard to his Oaths, which he made and broke with the very same Facility. The only Excuse that can be offered for him, is, that he had a View of Sovereignty from his

Infancy; little, and that but bad, Education in his Youth; and, after all, lived not long enough to attain any great Experience, which possibly might have made him better, and possibly also might have made him worse. His Reign was but of Fourteen Months, and in that Space he had little Quiet himself, allowed none to his Subjects; and with boundless Authority, and immense Riches, never excited Duty, or so much as acquired a single Friend, whose sage Advices might have prevented his sad Catastrophe. How insignificant then is Power! How destructive is Wealth! when they fall into the Hands of him, who only possesses that he may abuse them!

There was a Circumstance attending the Fate of *Suraja Dowlat*, that perhaps contributed to make even the Manner of it less regretted. Mr. *Law*, who had been formerly the *French* Chief at *Cassimbuzar*, a Gentleman, to do him Justice, of Honour and Abilities, had collected Two hundred of his Nation for the Service of the Suba, and was within a few Hours March of him when he was taken; upon hearing of which he stopped. This is a conclusive Proof that he was in his Pay, and a Circumstance that very fully justifies the *English* in their Conduct. If he had reached, and preserved *Suraja Dowlat*, the War would not have been so easily and so speedily finished. He who was without Friends in his Distress, might have again found Troops for Pay, or perhaps for Promises; so that his Death in this Respect had a stronger Air of Policy, and contributed to add Credit to the Report, that his Successor was not so entire a Stranger to it as he seemed. This Event likewise made it evident, that the Article which provided against the Return of the *French* into *Bengal*, was not either improper or imprudent. Colonel *Clive*, who sees Things and their Consequences in an Instant, detached Captain *Coote*, then of Colonel *Aldercron*'s Regiment, with Two hundred *Europeans*, and Five hundred Seapoys, in Pursuit of Mr. *Law*; and though that Force was fully sufficient, yet he engaged the Suba to send also Two thousand of his Horse, that his own Subjects and all *India* might know, that the *French* were equally his Enemies and Our's, and that being accustomed, from his first Entrance on Government, to fulfil his Engagements, he might learn to place his own Grandeur in adhering to his Word, and expect the Safety of his Dominions from the punctual Performance of his Promises. A Lesson that could not be taught at a more convenient Time.

The setting up the new, or rather restoring the old Form of Rule, was entirely due to the *English*, and the Suba and his Subjects were alike sensible of it; which was a Point of equal Honour and Advantage to the Nation. It afforded a strong and glorious Proof, that we, who in so long a Course of Years had never given the least Trouble or Uneasiness to the Government, were yet able to do ourselves Justice, when there was no other way left to remain in Quiet. On the other Hand, all the Advantages gained were by the fair and open Method of a Treaty, in which the first and most difficult Part was performed by us, and not taken violently or by force of Arms; though at the same time it was evidently in our Power to have done it, if it had been at all in our Will. When, therefore, Colonel *Clive* and Mr. *Watts* applied themselves to the Suba, for the specific Performance of that Agreement, which he had made previous to his Accession, the Justice of their Demand was without Hesitation acknowleged. The State of the Treasury was laid before them in the most candid Manner, so as to leave them not the least Reason to doubt, that what *Roydoolub* mentioned as an Objection at the concluding of the Treaty, was a real matter of Fact; and from the Dissipation that had happened since, the Suba was not in a Condition to fulfil his Promises, and discharge all his Obligations at once. Besides, it was for the Interest of the *English*, as well as for the Reputation of the Company, to support the Government which had been the Work of their own Hands, and not leave a Prince whom they had raised to the Subaship, with a Treasury absolutely empty, since supposing this in their Power, it must have exceedingly distressed him, and no less disgraced them.

In this State of Things, the Proportion he made seemed too equitable to be rejected. He offered to pay down a third of the whole Sum, to make it up one Moiety in a very short Space of Time, and to discharge the Remainder by equal Payments, in the Space of Three Years. This, therefore, was accepted, from a moral Persuasion that he, who parted with one Half in Consideration of what had been done for him, would likewise pay the other Half in the limited Time, to secure Assistance, in case any thing more was to be done. These then were the real Motives to the Agreement, which indeed took its Rise from Necessity, a Law that maintains its Rights under every Government, and in all Climates. There is a known Custom throughout

India, and in that Country more than in any other Custom has the Force of a Law, that Ten *per Cent.* is paid as Treasury Fees upon all Sums received, which those Gentlemen had Weight enough with *Roydoolub* to reduce to Five; and by the Help of this Concession, every thing was very soon adjusted, and the complete Moiety came into the Company's Possession. The candid Reader will probably think that Colonel *Clive* and Mr. *Watts* did, upon this very momentous Occasion, all that it was in their Power to do, and this was also their Sentiment; for as soon as more was in their Power, they took care to improve the Opportunity for the common Benefit of all concerned. A conclusive Testimony of the Uprightness of their Intention, in the whole of this Transaction.

This wonderful Sunshine of Prosperity at *Calcutta* was suddenly overcast, by the Death of a Great Man, to whose Virtues and Abilities the Inhabitants were indebted, in a very high Degree, for all the Happiness they possessed. This was *Charles Watson*, Esq; Vice-Admiral of the Blue, whose amiable Qualities in private Life added Lustre to his public Character. His Sentiments were noble, generous, and humane, his Manners graceful, easy, and polite; no Gentleman was ever more capable of gaining the Esteem of those with whom he conversed, and no Officer ever understood better how to exercise the Benevolence and Sweetness of his own Disposition, without impairing his Authority. In his Station he was Active without Hurry; Vigilant, without seeming to be Busy; and, with an open Countenance, ever attentive to his Duty. His Orders were obeyed with Pleasure, because they were enforced by his Example; and he was himself ready to do more than he ever expected from others. His having the Command in that critical Conjuncture, was, from the Beginning, looked upon as a singular and signal Blessing to the *English* settled in the *Indies*; and every Action of his afterwards confirmed that Notion. No Wonder, then, that his Death was considered as a common Calamity, and his Loss regretted as a public Misfortune. He was interred on the Seventeenth of *August*, when an unfeigned Sorrow was plainly visible in the Face of every Inhabitant, and a voluntary universal Mourning expressed, in some Degree, the true Sense the People had of his Merit, and the Effects that had been derived to them from thence. Indeed, they had been inconsolable, but for the Hopes they had still left in Admiral

Pocock. Hopes! that did not deceive them, and which have been productive of new Honours to the *British* Flag.

It was to the Attention of the Administration at Home, that the Company and the Subjects of *Great Britain* in *India* owed these potent and timely Succours; and, which was of no less Consequence, the prudent and happy Choice of the Officers who commanded them. The *French*, though deficient elsewhere, had a considerable Naval Force in the *Indies*, and were for this Reason very confident of their Success in that Part of the World; in which, perhaps, they had not been deceived, if, upon the Demise of Vice-Admiral *Watson*, the Command had devolved upon an Officer of less Merit, or even upon an Officer whose Merit had been less known or less established than that of Mr. *Pocock.* As it was, the Spirits of *British* Subjects were not depressed, or those of the Enemy raised. They had already known and felt his Courage, and he made them very quickly sensible of the Extent of his Capacity. They saw him equally active and vigilant: Their Squadrons no sooner appeared, than they had his in View. He was the Guardian of all our Settlements, and the Bane of all their Armaments and Expeditions. His Sagacity defeated many of their Designs, his Dexterity and Dispatch disconcerted others, till, by his Victories, he ruined, not their Reputation only, but their Strength in *Asia*, as completely as other Admirals had done in *Europe* and *America.* These are Facts indisputable; and, as they are connected with our Subject, we may take the Liberty of mentioning them, without giving Offence to that Gentleman, whose Modesty renders him as amiable, as his other Virtues have made him conspicuous. But to return to our Subject.

All Infant Governments are in their very Nature subject to Disorders. The new Suba, soon after the Departure of Colonel *Clive*, felt sufficiently, that, contrary to the first flattering Appearances, his Administration was not thoroughly established. Some of the Nabobs in his Province, dubious of his Intentions towards them, made no great haste to acknowlege an Authority that might be prejudicial to their own; and in the *Indies*, this kind of Delay is ever considered as Disobedience. Besides, *Meer Jaffeir* remembered the Advice which the Colonel had given him at Parting, which was, to acquire a Reputation for Firmness from his earliest Actions, if he meant to taste

Quiet in the remaining Part of his Reign. He resolved, therefore, to employ his Forces against those, who, though they did not presume to question his Title, shewed, notwithstanding, a Reluctancy to acknowlege it. He found, however, a sudden Stop put to his Operations. At the Beginning, some of his Officers were intractable, and his Troops in general were unwilling to move. He was entitled by the Treaty to Assistance from the *English*, and, upon his making the Demand, Colonel *Clive* marched instantly to his Relief. His Forces were not numerous; but he brought with him a Reputation that carried with it a Persuasion that he was ever irresistible, and his very Presence in the Suba's Camp restored Obedience to that Prince. Colonel *Clive*, and Mr. *Watts* who attended him, took this Opportunity to solicit the assigning Funds for the Money that was still due, and obtained from the Suba, though not without some Difficulty, all that they desired.

They likewise desired, and obtained, that the Company's Grant of Lands might be extended Northward from *Culpee* to *Rangafullah*, which, besides the Augmentation of Territory, was in other Respects a Matter of Importance.

The Nabob of *Patna*, whose Name was *Ramnaram*, against whom this Expedition was made, upon the Approach of the Suba's Army, offered to submit, and to pay his Tribute regularly, if he was continued in his Government, and the Suba's Promise was guarantied by Colonel *Clive*. The Suba requested this as a Favour of the Colonel, and desired that he would write a Letter to the Nabob, which he accordingly did; and upon the Faith of that Letter, he came and made his Submission. The great Product of *Patna* is Salt-petre, about which there had been formerly continual Disputes between us and the *Dutch*. At present, it was in the Hands of neither; but was still a Monopoly under a Lease. Colonel *Clive* and Mr. *Watts*, who knew the Consequence of such an Acquisition to the *English*, proposed the giving it in Lease to them, at the same Rate, which would be no Prejudice to the Suba; and the Juncture being favourable, this Proposition was complied with likewise, by which the Company are annually Gainers of about Two Lack and a half of Rupees, or something more than Thirty thousand Pounds Sterling. It is evident, therefore, from these Instances, that no favourable Opportunity was let slip, no single Occasion lost, that could be turned to the

Company's Advantage.

This Expedition, as it effectually fixed the new Suba in that Dignity, naturally brings the Memoirs of this Revolution to their Period. We cannot, however, conclude without observing, that as there could not be any thing more melancholy than the Situation of the Company's Affairs, when the Settlement of *Calcutta* was overwhelmed and destroyed, so nothing can be more satisfactory than to contemplate the Advantages that have resulted from this Alteration to the *East India* Company, the private and particular Sufferers, and the *British* Subjects who either reside in, or may hereafter go and reside in, *Bengal*. In reference to the Company, the Treaty with the present Suba procured them an ample Indemnity, without tying them down to a Specification of Losses, which would have been not more impossible than improper. The Sum was such as became the Rank and Grandeur of him who gave, and was admirably tinted to the Situation and Services of those who received. The Point of Security is likewise fully provided for; the Settlement may be fortified in such a Manner as to remove all Apprehensions; at the same time that these mighty Concessions are made, they are made in a Method that renders them doubly valuable, not through Fear or Compulsion, but with all possible Marks of Confidence and Esteem. The Interests of the Company, and the Country Government, are declared to be the same; and to prevent any Suspicion of Alteration, they are allowed an unrivalled Superiority, and the Enemies of the one are to be of Course the Enemies of the other. There is a Provision, as far as such a Provision can be made, that this Conjunction of Interests shall not be temporary, but perpetual; since the Company is at Liberty to take whatever Measures shall seem most expedient for the Safety of her Settlements, which is as much as could be either expected or desired.

The Regard shewn, and the Provision made, for all Degrees of Persons, who suffered by the Subversion of the Colony, was equally equitable and honourable. The Company, and those who depended upon it, shared the good as well as the ill Fortune that attended the different Administrations in *Bengal*. There were many of the *European* Sufferers, who were absolutely ruined and undone; reduced from Opulence and Ease, to Misery and Want, by a sudden, unforeseen, and inevitable Misfortune. These were restored to the whole of what they had lost, which was a Benefit to themselves, and to their Creditors in other parts of *India* and in *Europe*. Besides, as many of them had acquired their Fortunes by their Industry, and had spent almost their whole Lives in this Climate, it was not only a Piece of Justice to recover for them what they had lost, but a Point of true Policy to prevent the Terror of their Fate from having a mischievous Operation in succeeding Times, which otherwise it might have had; and this too in many Respects. The extending this Restitution to the *Jentoows* and *Armenians*, was not only a very exemplary but a very generous Act of Benevolence, founded in Principle. At the same time that it attached the particular Persons who were relieved, it raised the Reputation of the Company. It revived the Spirits of those useful Inhabitants, and gave a new Spring to their Activity and Industry, which were not only salutary Consequences at the Time, but will be found more so in their Effects, and facilitate the Execution of those Designs, that will be hereafter mentioned. This Tenderness for other Nations, this laudable Desire that they should share in the Prosperity, who had been hurt by the Adversity of the *English*, might be set in a far stronger Light, if placed in Comparison with the Conduct of others, without stirring out of *India*; but as that would be invidious, it is better omitted.

This stupendious Revolution may be also considered as equally glorious and advantageous to the *British* Nation. We may be allowed to say, because the Fact cannot be disputed, that it is a signal Proof of the Utility of Maritime Empire. As Commerce carries the Subjects of *Britain* every where, *British* Subjects every where experience *British* Protection: There are no Limits to our Naval Power, but those by which the Creator has confined the Globe. The *East India* Company was saved, and her Affairs restored, by the Attention and Arms of that Government by which she was erected. Many of those, who would have totally lost the Fruits of long Labour and various Hardships, and who must have been Beggars if subject to any other Power, are again easy in their Fortunes, and some of them have already transported their Effects to their native Country; the proper Return for the Assistance they derived from her maternal Affection; and as these Events have distinguished the present Age and the present Administration, so their Effects will probably be felt in succeeding Times. The Company, by an Accession of Territory, has an Opportunity of making an ample Settlement; which, under proper Management, may be not only extremely serviceable to her, but also to the Nation; and having a Revenue from these Lands, the Mint at *Calcutta*, and the Lease of the Salt-petre at *Patna*, which amounts in the whole to One hundred thousand Pounds a Year, there is a Provision against future Dangers upon the Spot, and without farther Expence. These Benefits have clearly arisen from that Revolution, of which we have given an Account, and are due to those who conducted it. May the future Emoluments do the like Honour to those who shall hereafter have the Care of the Company's and the Nation's Concerns in the *Indies*!

FINIS.